Small-Space Gardens

By the Editors of Sunset Books
and Sunset Magazine

Lane Publishing Co.,
Menlo Park, California

Edited by Kathryn L. Arthurs

Design: Joe di Chiarro

Cover: Marigolds, lobelia, and large pots of boxwood topiary edge summer vegetables in this 28-by-30-foot city garden. Impatiens forms a colorful mass against the garden walls. Design: W. David Poot. Photographed by Norman A. Plate.

Photography and Artwork: All the photographs in this book were taken by Ells Marugg, with two exceptions: Robert G. Bander, page 69, bottom left; and Glenn Christiansen, page 53, bottom. Garden and landscape drawings are by Jim McConnell; how-to illustrations by Vernon Koski.

Editor, Sunset Books: David E. Clark

First Printing   January 1978

Contents

Plant Lists and Special Features

Small Can Be Beautiful

Go, little book, and wish to all
Flowers in the garden, meat in the hall,
A bin of wine, a spice of wit,
A house with lawns enclosing it,
A living river by the door,
A nightingale in the sycamore!
　　Underwoods, *Robert Louis Stevenson*

Plants are not alone in sometimes needing tender, loving care. So do gardeners who work at the extremes—those with too much land to tend and those whose room for gardening does not stretch out far enough. This book has been written to reassure the space-squeezed gardener that, with the right approach, small can become beautiful.

The plant lover who lives in an apartment, condominium, or on a tiny city lot where space is extremely limited will find helpful ideas in this book for making maximum use of minimum dimensions. Small spaces call for both careful garden design and judicious plant selection.

Even people who enjoy extensive grounds may benefit from the guidelines found in these pages. Their space may include odd-shaped pockets that conventional landscaping can't handle—or perhaps someone's lifestyle would be enhanced by adding a walled picture garden off a bedroom or bathroom.

In turning a small-space liability into a large-scale asset, some gardeners seeking a leisure retreat have adapted the Oriental idea of a pleasure

The Pueblo look—small courtyard, stark elegance
Small spaces have been pressed into service as gardens in many cultures, many eras. Here, the desert version: Main court of hand-crafted Mexican pavers adjoins second court through small, covered loggia at rear. Olive tree (right) will grow to shade court. Design: Tom Orchard.

Tiny Mediterranean gardens go up—up—up
The idea of container gardening on balconies has long been popular with European apartment dwellers. Vertical color flourishes in pots, hanging baskets, and planter boxes.

garden—an exquisite miniature landscape designed for contemplation and meditation. Others whose main goal is privacy have been influenced by the traditional European idea of sharply separating public and private space by enclosing gardens and patios for secluded outdoor living.

This book's organization covers garden areas most likely to lack space: entries, side yards, atriums, decks and balconies, rear yards, and city gardens. In some cases, larger gardens with features adaptable to small spaces have been illustrated.

The actual dimensions of a small space are not as important as where the space is located. A side yard garden 7 feet wide and 57 feet long presents more of a design challenge than a small 20 by 20-foot rear yard.

Dealing with small-space gardens requires a different look at plants. Those that grow best in confined areas either stay small naturally or can adapt well to diminished growing space. From among the many plants that meet these requirements, we have selected a few to recommend for specific garden uses: ground covers, page 25; plants to espalier, page 32; vines, page 34; small trees, page 42; plants to grow in or around garden pools, page 50; vegetables, page 54; shrubs, page 65; and colorful plants, page 73.

What's in front (sketch above) changes in back (sketch below)
*Don't be deceived by the identical façades of these Victorian row houses **(top)**. Their back yards tell a very different story **(bottom)**. In very narrow spaces, the owners have taken highly individual approaches to garden design. Garden at left is high on entertaining, low on maintenance. It eliminates lawn, fills space with two-level deck, brick paving, fountain area. Center garden features flagstone entry path, open lawn, trellis-covered deck at rear. You enter garden at right down broad stairway, cross octagonal, brick-paved island in central lawn to reach raised deck bordered by trees, shrubs.*

Within the frame, an exquisite garden
Oriental shoji screens open to reveal a limited section of a charming landscape scene. Plants in 15-foot-deep small garden include azaleas, pines, podocarpus. Trees from yard beyond fence extend garden visually.

Introduction **5**

Landscaping Guidelines
Design pointers for small-space gardens

Scaling down your design approach to fit the confines of a mini-garden does not mean bypassing the four basic landscaping principles of *unity, balance, proportion,* and *variety.*
• A garden where all the various elements work together visually has **unity.** Repeating plants or building materials helps tie a garden together. This unified look gives the small garden an uncluttered feeling and helps create an illusion of space.
• Grouping landscaping elements to accent the focal point in a garden provides **balance,** either formal or informal. Balance does not always mean symmetry. It means using mass, color, or form to create comparable visual weight on either side of a center of interest.
• Especially important in a small-space garden, **proportion** keeps the plants and structural elements in scale with both the house and the space available.
• The most difficult principle to apply to small spaces is **variety.** Since the number of plants must be limited, choose those that change with the seasons for variety, or use container plants.

This section will help you evaluate your needs in the outdoor space you will be dealing with. It includes ideas to help make your outdoor room a livable extension of your interior spaces.

Our England is a garden,
And such gardens are not made
By singing, "Oh, how beautiful!"
And sitting in the shade.
    The Glory of the Garden, *Rudyard Kipling*

Take a Close Look at the Small Space

A good way to begin your landscape plan is to take inventory of what you have to work with. The two most important elements to consider are your actual plot of land and your climate.

Your Outdoor Space. People with a small-space garden usually have little control over the position of their outdoor space or the direction it faces. They are committed to developing an outdoor room wherever the space is located. It's not uncommon to be faced with severe slopes, buildings on several sides, and existing trees and plants on other people's property. Fortunately, most of these situations can be coped with effectively, with just a little innovation and some perseverance.

The actual square footage in a small-space garden is not as important as how the space is distributed. If your 100 square feet falls in a 5 x 20-foot side yard, the possible uses will be more limited than if the space is a 10 x 10-foot plot.

Space located on a steep slope that requires a retaining wall (see page 47 for information on retaining walls) or terraced planting beds will also be restrictive. Sometimes your small space will need to do double duty, as in the case of an entryway that must double as the main patio.

Many of these possible small-space situations are discussed in succeeding sections, starting on page 18. Ideas for different ways of dealing with these spaces are shown in both art and photographs.

The sun. The path of the sun and its intensity through the seasons may help determine the location of your outdoor room and the plants you can grow. If you have a choice as to exposure, select the location that provides sun during the time of day you will use your outdoor space the most.

Generally, a north-facing patio will always be shaded. An east-facing patio receives morning sun and afternoon shade. A west-facing patio and a south-facing patio both have sun in the afternoon and early evening.

The seasons. Even though people living in mild-winter climates can use their outdoor areas more frequently than people living in severe climates, some climate problems can be modified to increase the number of days an outdoor room is usable.

During cool weather, windbreaks and screens help prevent wind from lowering temperatures further. They also lessen the wind's force. A solid overhead shelters the patio on rainy days. If winter light is a problem, use translucent plastic for the overhead to protect the patio from rain and let in needed light.

The wind. Though it's something you can't see, wind has a powerful effect on your outdoor space. It can markedly lower temperatures, steal water from plants and soil through evaporation, flatten and destroy young or unsupported plants, and make outdoor living downright uncomfortable. To determine which direction your prevailing winds come from, notice the "lean" of the trees in your neighborhood.

In order to modify the wind's effects, you should understand how wind works. Wind is like water; it flows over solid barriers like a wave, crashing down on the other side. While your house forms your biggest windbreak, the wind could spill over it and drop directly on the patio. Since solid barriers are not always the most effective, consider screens and windbreaks as possible solutions.

A fence with an open space at the bottom gives some wind control; the most protection comes at a distance equal to the fence's height. Adding a 45° baffle at the top of a fence eliminates the wind's downward thrust. Louvered or lath fences efficiently diffuse the wind's force.

Trees, hedges, and screens of dense foliage plants grown as windbreaks also control the wind. When wind hits trees and open shrubs, the plants allow some of it through, creating turbulence and breaking up the wind's force.

What Do You Want from Your Garden?

Well-designed gardens—both large and small—begin with decisions made before the first spadeful of earth is turned. Do you want an elegant, formal landscape or an outdoor room for casual living and entertaining? Do you want a lovely garden filled with specimen plants or a durable one that can withstand a game of tag or tricycle wheels? Do you like to read and sunbathe or play badminton or croquet? Do you enjoy gardening or do you prefer to enjoy the garden with a minimum of effort? Do you want to produce fresh fruits and vegetables? Is privacy a priority item? Answering these questions and carefully evaluating your lifestyle will help determine what you want in your outdoor space.

Keep in mind that there are limits to what a small-space garden can include. Make a checklist of items that are essential to you and include them in your landscape plan. Be prepared to compromise on the less important elements.

How to Plan Your Garden Design

In working out your landscape plan, consider some strategies used by landscape architects. They design a garden generously, then figure the costs. A 5-foot-wide brick walk will be far more expensive than a 3-foot-wide walk, but the additional width adds a scope and creates a feeling of luxury.

Another trick landscape architects use is to create a bold design. With a strong design that makes a definite statement, plant growth in future years cannot erase the original plan.

In organizing space, most designers rely on familiar shapes, such as the square, the rectangle,

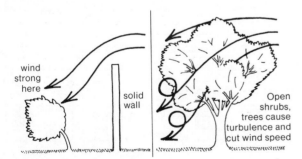

Foliage can control the wind
Strong winds tumble over top of solid wall, batter plants (left). Trees, tall plants in path of prevailing winds let some wind through to lessen force (right).

Squares

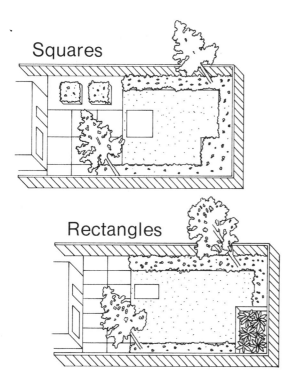

Rectangles

Triangles

Circles

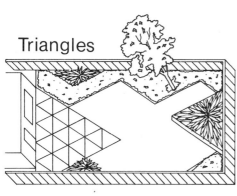

Base pleasing garden design on familiar shapes

Most people find a sense of order in well-known shapes. The four garden plans shown above were designed around easily recognizable forms: squares, rectangles, triangles, circles.

the triangle, the hexagon, and the circle. Many design variations are possible using these shapes.

Use your design to guide people to the areas you'd like them to see. Your entry walk should invite guests to the front door. If you have a second sitting area away from the main patio, an interesting path should lead to it. Another useful idea is to hide parts of your landscape behind plants or a screen. A path that disappears behind a garden wall encourages exploration.

Put your plan on paper. The first step in creating a garden design is to make a scale drawing of your lot and house. Make a large plan on graph paper to show exactly what you have to work with. Use the largest scale the graph paper will allow; a common scale is ¼ inch equaling 1 foot.

Here are some things to include on the plot plan:
• Give dimensions of the lot.
• Indicate which way is north.
• Show the direction of prevailing winds.
• Locate easements that could affect your plan, such as underground telephone or power lines and sewers.
• Indicate setback boundaries. These can be checked with your local building department.
• Locate utilities—water, gas, and sewers—and depths of each; underground wires; outlets on outside of house for water, electricity, meter boxes.
• Place house on lot with access shown—doors and windows and the rooms they open from.
• Give gradient information—show contour lines; locate high and low spots, natural drainage that affects your lot, downspouts.
• Show existing plants, especially established trees.
• Note any problems beyond the lot line, such as

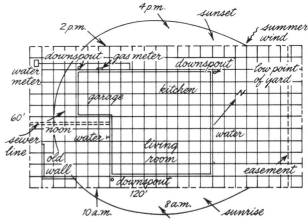

Scale drawing of lot

Make a sketch of your lot on graph paper for plot plan, showing what you have to work with.

favorable or unfavorable views of neighbor's property, hills, trees, power poles.

Once you complete this plot plan, bring out the list of items you'd like to include in your outdoor space. Place tracing paper over your plot plan. Then begin to design. (The tracing paper allows you to keep the original plan intact. If you make an error, just pull out another piece of tracing paper and start again.)

In the sample design shown below, circles were used as the basic theme. Work with the various areas until you have included all your items and the design suits you.

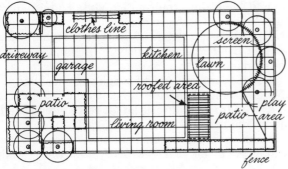

Garden plan marked on tracing paper
Sample garden design is done on tracing paper laid over plot plan; circles used as design elements.

Do you need professional advice? Your outdoor space may present problems, such as a very steep slope or a severe wind problem, that can best be solved by an expert. Landscape architects and designers can deal with awkward spaces, giving expert advice on both plants and overall design. Landscape contractors, in addition to overseeing the actual construction of patios, overheads, retaining walls, and fences, can also give useful advice.

If a steep slope or poor drainage are problems, you may want to consult a structural engineer.

Structural Elements

Once you have your landscape design on paper, you will need to select materials for walks and patio surfaces, fences and screens, and overheads. You will also need to choose furniture and plan for outdoor lighting.

The following section deals with the various materials and products available. Plan to select materials that are durable, pleasing to the eye, and

in line with your budget. (The actual installation of each structure or material is not covered.)

Patio floors and walks. Make an effort to select a surfacing material that both fits the style of your garden and works with the architecture of your house. Using materials that are available locally will be more practical than choosing those that must be imported.

Brick fits almost any design situation, is widely available, and is easy for a novice to install. Many brick textures and colors are available: textures vary from rough to almost smooth and colors range from fawn to ebony. Used brick, salvaged from old buildings and walls, can add a rustic look if used sparingly. You can also find manufactured used brick.

You can set bricks either in sand or mortar in many different patterns. Setting bricks in sand is easier for the beginner and will be permanent in areas where the ground does not freeze.

Concrete, a very versatile material, can be finished plain and smooth, rough textured, patterned, or blended with exposed aggregate. You can combine it with other materials easily and cast it in endless shapes and forms. Concrete patios and walks may be finished off with colors.

Concrete does have some disadvantages: it is a hard surface, absorbing heat in the summer and cold in winter. Because it is porous, concrete shows stains.

Outdoor floor tiles are rough-surfaced, contrasting with the glazed tiles used indoors. They provide a finished look, effectively joining indoor and outdoor areas. Tile comes in several sizes and colors.

Flagstone seems appropriate in natural garden settings. The harder types of flagstones form a permanent surface and will survive in winter where bricks sometimes fail. If you live in severe winter areas, be sure to order hard flagstone. Slabs are irregular in shape and thickness. They can be put directly on soil or set in mortar.

Rock and *gravel* work well for paths, play yards, and service and storage areas. They come as manmade, crushed rock or natural, rounded gravel. A standard size for use on paths is ½-inch crushed gravel.

Because gravel may settle into the soil or be scattered, it will have to be replenished from time to time. You will need to rake it occasionally to maintain an even surface.

Bark is a very natural material. Reddish brown in color, it is soft and springy to walk on and not harmed by moisture. Since it scatters easily, confine it with header boards.

Wood adds a warm color and soft texture to the garden. It will not last as long as concrete or stone. Most woods can be treated with preservatives or be pressure-treated to add years of life.

Garden screens and fences. A fence, planting materials, or a combination of the two can enclose your outdoor space. If you want immediate privacy, a 6-foot-high fence is your solution.

Wood fence designs come in many varieties—grapestake, slat, louvered, board, lattice or basketweave, and solid wood panels. Choose the design that best meets your needs. Grapestakes, split from redwood or cedar logs, are lightweight, easy to install, and resistant to decay. A slat fence is more formal and helps control wind. Louvered fences help control sunlight, wind, and privacy.

Board and solid wood panel fences give maximum privacy and go up quickly, but they also create a boxed-in feeling. To break the monotony, boards can be spaced or formed in a basketweave or lattice pattern.

Fiberglass and *plastic* panels come flat or corrugated. Placed in a frame, they are durable and provide privacy without shutting out light.

Chain-link fencing is visually open. Its commercial look can be disguised with plants or vines.

Hedges and *dense plantings* can also serve as screens or enclose the outdoor room. However, they may take several years to reach screening size.

Solid masonry walls of *brick* or *stone* will also serve the purpose, but they are very expensive.

Providing an overhead. Overheads increase the usability of your patio or terrace by providing protection from sun, wind, and rain.

Trees form beautiful and natural roofs, but small spaces have size limits (see the list of trees suitable for small spaces on page 42).

Structural overheads provide immediate protection. If an overhead is attached to the house, it should blend into the house's style and architecture. A free-standing roof allows greater latitude in overhead design. Types of overheads include lath, reed or bamboo, canvas, plastic, aluminum, or louvered panels.

A *lath* overhead—wood strips spaced at various distances and supported by beams and crosspieces—can be freestanding or attached to the house. It filters the sun and wind.

Reed or *bamboo* make effective screens but will have to be replaced every few years. They

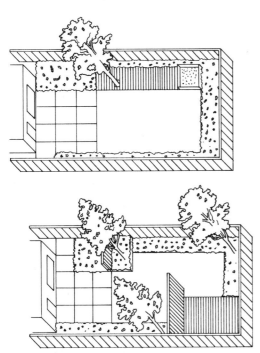

Screens can make all the difference

In open garden design **(top)**, *everything is visible at first glance.* **Bottom:** *When parts of garden are hidden by offset screens, the space seems larger. Concealed parts of garden tempt guests to explore, offer private nooks.*

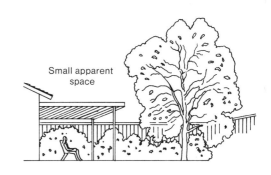

Small apparent space

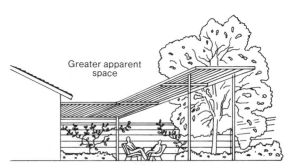

Greater apparent space

Enlarged overhead increases apparent space

Typical square overhead **(top)**, *dense foliage against fence give garden closed-in appearance.* **Bottom:** *Larger, right-angled roof directs eye outward, makes garden appear more spacious. Espaliered plants on fence add to open feeling.*

provide densely filtered shade and a more natural shade pattern than lath.

Canvas will withstand the sun, wind, and rain, but it retards air movement. It is lightweight, requiring less support than wood overheads.

Wood louvers can be permanent or adjustable. Set permanently at an angle, they block the sun at certain times of the day. Adjustable louvers can be moved to control the sun at any time.

Plastic panels are available in many colors and textures. Translucent, they let in some light but keep out the wind and rain. Plastic needs a frame for support.

Corrugated aluminum, available in many colors, gives complete protection. It may be noisy when the wind blows, however, and it expands and contracts with heat and cold, loosening attachments.

Garden furniture. You can choose between two types of furniture: built-in tables and benches, and free-standing furniture. Built-in furniture should be included in the initial garden design; you can add pieces of free-standing furniture at any time.

Built-in benches and tables work well in small spaces. Since benches are attached, they take up less floor space than chairs. They can double as counters or plant container displays, and they can also serve as part of a retaining wall. Since built-ins are permanent, choose building materials that can withstand your climate extremes.

Free-standing furniture comes in wood (usually redwood), wrought iron, steel, painted or enameled aluminum frame with plastic webbing, and plastic. If the furniture you choose cannot withstand your winters, be sure you have enough storage space to accommodate it. All types of free-standing furniture come in a wide range of styles and colors.

Garden lighting. Whether you are lighting walkways for safety, spotlighting favorite plants, or illuminating the garden area for nighttime entertaining, certain basic rules will apply:

1. In small spaces, you should normally see the light but not the source. Unless the fixture is decorative, don't let it compete with the garden. A glimpse of utilitarian metal could spoil the magical quality of night lighting.

2. Try not to provide too much light, giving the garden a white-washed look. Use several small lights instead of two or three powerful ones.

3. When accenting plants, take both the plant and the light source into consideration. Spotlighting a plant creates drama and lets you see the plant clearly; on the other hand, silhouetting shows the plant's shape and outline. Plants with translucent foliage take on a special look when backlighted. You can also create a shadow play by casting plant shapes onto walls or fences.

Outdoor lighting systems offer two choices: low voltage (12 volts) and standard voltage (120 volts). Before you install either system, check with your local building department to see if you need a building permit. Most cities follow the National Electric Code requirements, but some areas have added amendments and restrictions.

A low-voltage system may be your best bet in a small-space garden. It is safe and easy to install, even for a beginner, and will be most effective in small areas. Several low-voltage fixtures are pictured below.

Low-voltage fixtures to light up your landscape

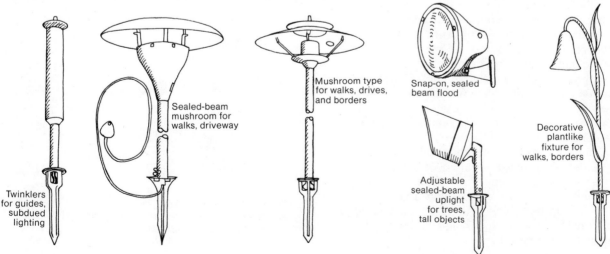

Twinklers for guides, subdued lighting

Sealed-beam mushroom for walks, driveway

Mushroom type for walks, drives, and borders

Snap-on, sealed beam flood

Adjustable sealed-beam uplight for trees, tall objects

Decorative plantlike fixture for walks, borders

Basic Gardening for Small Spaces
From soils to soakers

Though the techniques of gardening in small spaces are the same as those followed in larger gardens, mini-gardens are much less time-consuming. But a small garden has its own special demands. Here, your plants will always be in the limelight. Because of this, the effects of plant disease, pests, or poor care can be devastating to the garden's image.

Whether you plant directly in the ground or in raised beds or containers, you'll get the best results if you follow these basics of soil preparation, watering, fertilizing, and general garden maintenance.

". . . but we must cultivate our garden."
Candide, *Voltaire*

Good Soil Makes the Difference

Soil is the most important ingredient in successful small-space gardening. If you have serious soil problems, consider planting only in raised beds or containers where you can carefully control the soil mix (see pages 56-57 for information on growing plants in containers).

Soils come in two basic types: heavy clay or sandy. Heavy soil, called clay or adobe, is easy to recognize but difficult to work with. You can squeeze a handful together, and you'll get a gummy plastic mass that won't break apart even if you tap it with a shovel. Though clay soil is often rich, it contains very little space for air; plant roots may drown from lack of oxygen. Clay soils do have this advantage: slow drainage prevents nutrients from leaching out.

Compared to clay soil, sandy soil has huge particles that allow good aeration, quick passage of water, and rapid temperature changes. Sandy soil provides plenty of air for plant roots, and the roots can spread easily. But here's the rub: water will pour right through, taking any plant nutrients you've applied with it.

To improve soil quality, you can buy all new topsoil and spread it over your area. Or you can add mineral or organic amendments to improve the soil you already have. Since small spaces can be awkward to reach, think about how you'll get new topsoil or soil amendments into your garden before you order. If the only way to reach your rear postage-stamp-size patio is over the white living

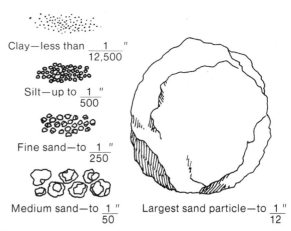

Clay—less than $\frac{1}{12,500}$"

Silt—up to $\frac{1}{500}$"

Fine sand—to $\frac{1}{250}$"

Medium sand—to $\frac{1}{50}$"

Largest sand particle—to $\frac{1}{12}$"

Soil types range from clay to sand
Soil type depends on size of particles it contains. Clay soil is made up of small, tightly packed particles. Sandy soil consists of larger particles with tiny air pockets between.

room carpet, you won't want to order a truckload of topsoil.

Mineral amendments such as pumice, perlite, or vermiculite break down slowly by weathering. Usually considered too expensive for large area treatments, mineral amendments may be just the answer for small patches of problem soil.

Organic amendments like ground bark, peat moss, or leaf mold improve dense clay soils by physically separating the fine clay particles without holding moisture. To improve sandy soil, you should add a spongy organic amendment, such as peat moss. Spongy particles fill the open spaces between the sand particles, helping retain moisture and nutrients.

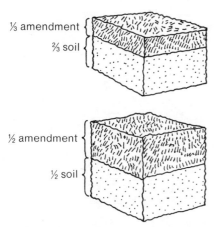

Amendments make soil richer

To improve soil, spread amendment layer over soil, then mix in thoroughly. Final soil mix should contain ⅓ amendment for normal soils, ½ amendment for clay soils.

When you add any type of amendment to your soil, add enough to equal 25 to 50 percent of the total soil volume. Mix in amendments thoroughly and deeply.

Soil Nutrition

In addition to light, air, water, and root room, growing plants need a supply of nutrients—elements necessary to carry out their life processes. Small amounts of some essential elements should already be present in your soil, but most gardeners will need to supplement the three major elements—nitrogen, phosphorus, and potassium—by adding a chemical or organic fertilizer. These major elements are crucial to normal plant growth: nitrogen promotes rapid growth of stems and leaves and gives plants a deep green color; phosphorus en-

courages root formation, flowers, and fruit; potassium aids in root growth and seed production and is instrumental in all plant functions.

You can fertilize your plants with either chemical or organic fertilizers. Organic fertilizers—cotton seed meal, blood meal, and bone meal, for example—give up their nutrients slowly, since bacterial action is required before nutrients can be released. However, organics don't contain all the needed trace elements. Chemical fertilizers come in dry, liquid, or tablet forms. Those containing the three main elements plus the necessary trace elements are called complete fertilizers. Labels on packaged fertilizers give instructions for their use; be sure to follow them carefully.

Before you buy a fertilizer, check to see how much of these major elements it contains. Somewhere on the fertilizer package, you'll find three numbers, such as 10-8-6. In a 10-pound bag with these numbers, 10 percent is nitrogen, 8 percent is phosphorus, 6 percent is potassium, and the rest of the material is inert.

Special Soil Problems

Poor plant performance, despite good care, may mean you have a special soil problem. The following list includes the most common soil problems with possible solutions:

Alkalinity. Alkaline soil, common in light rainfall areas, is high in calcium carbonate (lime) and other minerals. Many plants grow well in moderately alkaline soil, though acid-loving plants will not. You can avoid the high alkalinity problem by planting in raised beds and in containers filled with a prepared soil mix.

Acidity. Acid soil is most common in heavy rainfall areas. Since all acid soils have low levels of calcium (lime), ground limestone will help neutralize an acid-reacting soil. If you do add lime, be sure to use a fertilizer that won't increase soil acidity. Some plants—azaleas, rhododendrons, and camellias, for example—prefer moderately acid soil.

Salinity. This condition is a widespread problem in arid and semiarid regions. A high concentration of salts in the root zone area can prevent germination, stunt plant growth, and turn leaves yellow or brown (salt burn).

Periodic and thorough leaching will lessen the salt content. To leach plants in the ground, let a hose run at a slow trickle for several hours at the base of the plant stem. To leach plants in containers, water until excess runs out the drainage holes, let it drain, then rewater.

Chlorosis. If the leaves of some plants turn yellow while the veins stay green, the plants may be deficient in iron. Chelating (pronounced key-lating) agents or iron sulfate can control chlorosis; buy either at a nursery or garden supply store. Be sure to follow label directions carefully.

Shallow soil or hardpan. A layer of hardpan within the top 18 inches of your soil layer stops water penetration and keeps roots from growing. To counteract it, you can drill through shallow hardpan to make a vertical gravel drain or get advice from an engineer on how to install drain tiles horizontally. Switching to raised beds and containers will also solve the problem.

Man-made hardpan exists where heavy construction equipment has compacted soil, making claylike subsoil brick-hard when dried. To remedy this condition, you can grow a crop of deep-rooted grass—annual rye, for example—and plow it under before adding amendments. Again, switching to raised beds and containers solves this problem.

A Word to the Wise on Water

The trick to proper watering is to use just the right amount—too much water can be just as dam-

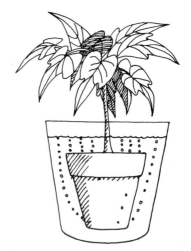

Periodic plunge—a good way to water
Submerge plant and container into larger basin of water and wait for bubbling to stop. This insures constant moisture throughout root ball.

Pebble mulch conserves water
To keep soil moist longer, set potted plant inside large container, fill space between with damp peat. Cover soil, peat with layer of small pebbles.

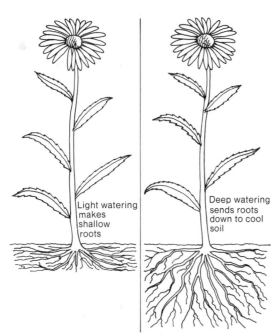

Light watering makes shallow roots

Deep watering sends roots down to cool soil

Deep watering encourages proper root growth
Frequent, light watering wets only upper few inches of soil, makes roots stay near surface (left). Soaking soil more completely promotes deeper root growth (right).

Group plants to beat the heat
During warm weather, container plants hold moisture better if grouped together. Set plants on gravel bed that's kept constantly moist.

aging as too little. If you keep watering chores to a minimum, the watering you do will reach the plant roots instead of evaporating.

Most plants get their moisture from the soil layers near the surface. Only a few plants, mainly grasses and trees, have roots that reach down into the deeper layers. But the surface layers of soil are constantly losing water. Plants take it up through their roots and release it through their leaves during the day, particularly in hot weather. Moisture also evaporates because of dry winds and the sun heating the ground. These causes of water loss are most evident in hot climates with long, dry seasons.

In general, frequent, shallow watering is ineffective because it encourages roots to stay close to the upper few inches of moist soil. You waste water and time since surface moisture evaporates quickly. Frequent, shallow watering also produces more shallow-rooted weeds and encourages fungus and disease organisms.

A good basic watering plan is to soak the soil deeply, then wait until the top few inches of soil begin to dry out before watering again. This way, plant roots will be encouraged to grow into deeper soil layers where they will stay cool; weeds with shallow roots won't have a chance to grow.

How much water will you need for deep watering? Enough to exceed the holding capacity of the top layer of soil so that water will be forced to penetrate. Porous soil particles such as sand hold less water than fine clay soil particles. In average loam, 1 inch of water will penetrate 6–10 inches; in sand, 12 inches; in clay, only 4–5 inches. To check the degree of water penetration in your soil, first water, then wait a day or two and dig up a spadeful of soil.

Frequent, deep watering will be as bad as shallow watering. Such overwatering cuts off oxygen to plant roots, drowning plants or making roots more susceptible to fungus diseases.

How you apply water can be as important as how often and how long you water. When you water by hand, take it easy. A spray mist nozzle attached to your hose or a fine-spray watering can is the gentlest—a strong jet of water digs holes in the soil and exposes roots. Some hand watering devices and hose accessories are shown below.

To save time, you can install a drip irrigation system consisting of plastic or metal pipes with holes drilled at intervals to drip, bubble, or squirt water onto plants or into containers. A drip system can also be placed on a timer, a real boon for people who travel frequently.

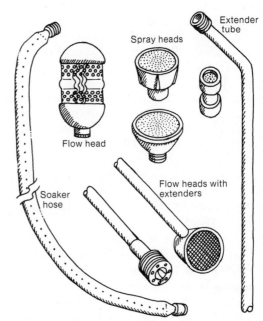

Hose-end nozzles do varied jobs

These nozzles do specific watering jobs. Clockwise: pistol washes plants with hard bursts; adjustable barrel changes from fine mist to hard spray; fan waters beds, containers; sweeper, fire hose good for lawns, washing pavement; mister increases humidity.

Seven soakers for canny watering

Soakers supply water without gouging holes in soil. **Left to right:** Soaker hose *of plastic or canvas (place holes up for mist, down for soak).* Flow heads *release large volume of water.* Spray heads *emit generous, coarse spray.* Heads with extender tubes *for watering wide beds, hanging baskets.*

Establish Good Gardening Habits

No plant is immune to pests or plant diseases, but you can reduce the risk of an attack by following these good gardening practices:

1. Keep your garden free of weeds, dead flowers, and fallen leaves and fruit.

2. Replace plants that show signs of disease year after year with disease-resistant varieties. Burn or discard diseased plants.

3. If annuals show signs of disease year after year, try a different annual next season. Some disease organisms can remain in the soil and ruin the same annual next year. Or avoid soil diseases altogether by planting in containers or raised beds filled with a sterilized soil mix.

4. Give plants the proper growing conditions. Don't crowd them—doing this will cut down on air circulation.

5. Remove plants after their normal growing season and before they're past their prime. Old and weak plants are especially prone to disease.

6. Keep soil in good shape by regularly adding soil amendments and nutrients.

Those pesky pests

The following list contains some of the most common garden pests as well as simple ways to eradicate them. Learn to recognize these pests and the signs of their inroads on your plants.

Aphids. Pests with soft, round bodies, usually green or reddish black. Live and feed in colonies; stunt plant growth; spread diseases. You can get rid of them by rubbing them off, hosing them off, or washing the plant with soapy (not detergent) solution.

Beetles. Many kinds and sizes; feed on leaves, bark. Hand pick the large, slow-moving ones. Kill grubs (larvae) in the soil if you turn them up while cultivating.

Borers. Larvae (caterpillars or grubs) bore into stems and trunks. Paint special adhesive around tree base to kill pests on their way up the trunk.

Caterpillars. Larvae of moths and butterflies; some smooth, others hairy; great variation in size. Most chew leaves. Squash them or put them in a paper bag and burn it.

Slugs and snails. Feed at night and on cool, overcast days; leave trails of silvery slime. Place boards out at night; turn them over every morning, and squash snails or discard boards in a plastic bag.

Spider mites. Bad summer pests; detectable only in groups or by stippled leaves with silvery webs on the underside. Isolate infested plants. Wash mites off with soapy (not detergent) solution.

Thrips. Tiny insects that often fly when disturbed and feed on foliage and flowers. Hose them off.

Whiteflies. Small, white flying pests that attach and feed on undersides of leaves. Foliage turns yellow and is covered with shiny, sticky honeydew. Hose off or apply a soapy (not detergent) solution.

If these methods won't control pests, ask your nurseryperson for advice on chemical controls. Before applying any chemical, carefully read the label instructions. When you've finished the application, thoroughly wash your equipment, clothing, and hands or other exposed skin. Store the chemical and any measuring device you use in a locked cabinet.

Dealing with Plant Diseases

Some common plant diseases and suggested treatments are listed below, roughly in the order in which they most frequently occur. If a diseased plant resists your treatment, get rid of it. Some diseases spread quickly to neighboring plants.

Powdery mildew. A gray or white dust that appears on leaves, stems, and flower buds. Discard infected annuals; cut off diseased parts of permanent plants. Chemical controls are acti-dione and benomyl.

Verticillium wilt. This disease lives in the soil and frequently attacks tomatoes. Leaves turn yellow and brown, die from the base of the plant upward. No spray is effective; plant wilt-resistant tomato varieties.

Damping off. Newly sprouted seedlings develop a stem rot near the soil surface and fall over (or the seeds never sprout). Bake containers of soil before sowing seeds. Chemical controls are dexon and streptomycin.

Root rots, water molds. Diseases caused by water mold fungi usually involve container plants. Chemical control is difficult; prevent these diseases with good soil preparation, good drainage, and careful watering.

Botrytus, gray mold. Epidemics develop under cool, moist conditions with high humidity. Symptoms are soft decay of flowers, leaves, or stems, followed by a covering of downy gray mold. Quickly remove dead plant parts or use chemical controls (benomyl, folpet, zineb) at the first sign of disease.

Keep Your Plants in Trim

Pruning becomes an important chore in a small-space garden. When you're dealing with a limited area that's always on view, you'll want to keep plants small and well shaped. Pruning also keeps plants healthy and can increase quality and yield of flowers and fruit.

Before you start to pinch or prune plants, you need to know about terminal buds, the growing buds located at branch ends. These tip buds add length to branches by drawing energy from the plant during active growth.

Pinching off branch tips signals the plant to produce new branches at other buds. To change the direction a branch is growing, find a fat bud growing in the direction you prefer, then snip off the whole branch just above that bud. The bud will take over. Remember: it's better for the plant and its shape if the new branch can grow toward an open space rather than toward another branch.

Tip-pinch for bushy plants
When you pinch out growing tip (terminal bud) of plant with your thumb and forefinger, it forces development of side shoots or branches. Frequent tip-pinching keeps plants bushy, well-shaped, helps avoid heavy pruning later.

An important pruning rule to keep in mind is never to make a cut at an arbitrary point along a branch. Cut just above a bud or a good branch or make the cut flush with the trunk or base. If you cut between two buds leaving a stub, no nourishment will pass through the tissue between the cut, causing the bud and the stub to die. Decay and insects can enter the plant through the dead stub.

Generally, plants need some kind of pruning just before or at the beginning of the growing season. Fruit trees and roses have special pruning rules; major pruning is usually done in late winter when branches are bare.

Shrubs and trees that produce flowers can be pruned after flowers fade and just as new leaf growth is beginning. If you grow a plant specifically for cut flowers, cut off blooms at spots where the plant's shape is retained and you have a reasonably long stem. Remove stubs and inferior branches.

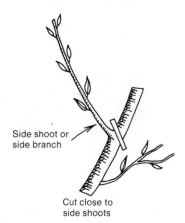

Side shoot or side branch

Cut close to side shoots

Where to make a pruning cut
When pruning, make angular cut only above a bud or side shoot, close to juncture. Never leave a stub. If possible, choose a bud or side shoot that points in the direction you'd like new growth to take.

Two basic pruning tools are a pruning saw (the curved folding saw is best for a beginner—and it stores easily) and a sturdy pair of pruning shears. Your hands are "tools," too. As you walk around the garden, pinch back spindly shoots, rub out unwanted buds along stems, and snap off faded blooms and seed pods.

For specific pruning directions for each plant, see Sunset's *Pruning Handbook.* And Sunset's *Basic Gardening Illustrated* has more information on all aspects of gardening.

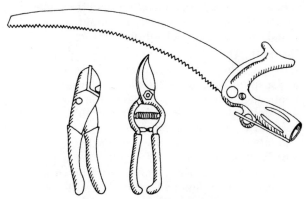

Three pruning tools for small-space gardeners
Hand pruning shears are basic tools. Both types do all light jobs. Curved pruning saw easily cuts through green wood, can be attached to wooden or metal telescoping pole for trees, tall shrubs.

Entry Gardens
Greening up the front door

First impressions can be important. And when first-time guests arrive, your entry garden should guide them to the front door and invite them to go in. Attractive plantings, adequate lighting, and a smooth, safe pathway are basics. Containers filled with colorful or unusual plants, or an interesting piece of garden art, can lend a stamp of individuality.

In some instances, your entry garden will be the only outdoor space you have available. In this case, it will need to double as a patio or outdoor room. You will want to achieve some privacy for your entertaining and still maintain an attractive entryway.

Unlock the door this evening
*   And let your gate swing wide,*
Let all who ask for shelter
*   Come speedily inside.*
*   Gates and Doors, Joyce Kilmer*

Your Doorway to the World

Let's begin by looking at the basics: a good entry includes an inviting path that leads to the main entrance, adequate lights for nighttime visitors, and plantings that soften and accent the house and its surroundings. Since the entry introduces guests to your home, it should reflect the style and atmosphere of the house and contain some individual touches that make it distinctive.

The path. Unless your front door opens directly onto the sidewalk or driveway, a path becomes a landscaping tool to tie the various structural elements together visually, dividing the garden into well defined areas. Whenever possible, plan for width in walks and porch areas.

Plants that border walks and porches should be kept well-pruned to avoid obstructing a path or snagging clothes. Keep shrubs and flowers with thorns or sharp edges well out of the traffic pattern.

Two factors should influence your choice of paving materials: cost and compatibility. You should look for materials that will accent the style and structure of your home. Brick paving is a common choice for traditional houses; more contemporary

homes often look best with a wide walk of wooden decking or exposed aggregate paving. If a paved area is extensive, try to carve out softening areas for planting islands.

Before selecting the material for a path, estimate the amount you'll need, its cost, and the cost

Color up a green garden
Portable containers of brightly colored tulips add interest to predominantly green garden in small entryway space. Carefully placed wooden boxes and tubs visually lead guests to front door.

Entry walk grows into patio

Brick combined with concrete softens paving, echoes house exterior. Patio is arranged into small conversation areas, screened from street by cypress hedge. Design: W. David Poot.

...Entry Gardens

of installation. Local building materials are usually less expensive than materials that are shipped from other areas. Don't set your heart on polished marble if your budget says aggregate paving. Further information on walks can be found on pages 9-10.

Garden lighting. Lights in the entry can be both functional and decorative. Essential lights will lead guests safely from the street to the door. Steps or path irregularities should be well lit, as well as the doorbell and street numbers or name plates.

Extra lighting can serve as garden accents; the entry is a good place to create drama after dark. Spotlighting special or unusual plants that have interesting shapes or leaf or branch patterns can give your entry special appeal.

What about the plants? Plants in entry gardens serve several functions. They are the glue that holds the landscape together. They soften or draw attention away from harsh or mundane structures. They provide color and texture, and they screen out unpleasant views and create privacy.

The best advice for choosing plants for an entry garden is to plan simply. Limit the types of permanent plants to a select few. Shrubs and ground covers, including lawns, form the foundation; colorful annuals and a tree or two serve as accents.

Streetside patio at entry offers cool desert living

*Entry seating area (**above**) was designed to take advantage of three existing, large, fruitless mulberry trees that provide needed shade during hot summer and let in warming sun through leafless winter branches. Seating area is partially hidden from street by 3-foot concrete block wall, purposely kept low to open patio to cooling summer breezes. Tall concrete block wall section topped with beams blocks front door from public view, separates entry and seating areas. **Below:** L-shaped wooden screen contributes to privacy by hiding driveway, minimizing view of traffic on busy street. Patio floor is brick set in sand in basketweave pattern. Plants in containers add movable color. Design: Thomas C. Zimmerman.*

Seclusion in a lush green entry

Tiny hideaway seating area in entry: a built-in bench backed by wooden fence panels. Patio garden also provides enclosed view from living room. Varied baffle of slats, boards at left screens traffic. Plants blend many shades of green to soften exposed aggregate paving. Design: John Herbst, Jr.

Containers create island of color in entry courtyard

Colorful entry (above) doesn't restrict variety of plants grown by avid gardener. Placing plants in containers limits their natural spread, allows more room for diversity. Climbing roses, daylilies, ground covers fill narrow beds along fence, forming background for banks of summer annuals in containers. Potted plants in center of display are raised on low platform for maximum exposure. Brick paving in diagonal herringbone pattern can be hosed down to raise humidity for plants. **Right:** *Alternate board fence hides entry from street. Small bed between gate and garage is thickly planted with camellias, ferns, daisies, marigolds, and other summer annuals.*

Brick wall, foliage frame space for outdoor dining

Tiny entry enclosed by U-shaped brick wall painted pumpkin creates room for outdoor meals. Wall color matches house, is compatible with red brick paving, plants. Hydrangeas, rhododendrons are permanent, accented by transient pots of geraniums, jade, liriope. Design: Robert W. Chittock.

...Entry Gardens

Use a tree or a specimen shrub with flowers, berries, or striking foliage as a focal point. Since your entry will be on view year-round, evergreen plants are a good choice.

Maintenance should also be a consideration when selecting plants for small-space entries. A plant that is messy or that requires lots of pruning may not be the best choice. Position plants with thorns, spiky leaves, or rough bark in a less public portion of your garden, away from walkways. Seasonal color can be used in containers or placed in the ground as borders around permanent plants.

The Entry Patio

When your entry has to do double duty as a patio or outdoor room, some unique problems arise. You will want to entertain family and friends without

A plant facelift for this townhouse's stacked entries
Wrought iron gate leads into lower doorway opening directly onto busy city sidewalk. Door below is flanked by well-trimmed podocarpus (evergreen, easy to control, attractive year-round). Brick-edged sidewalk planting bed contains low boxwood hedge, chrysanthemums, seasonal color. Upper porch made more inviting by containers painted black to match house's trim. Design: Robert C. Chesnut.

Tree branch adds importance to understated front door
Opening directly into driveway on side of house, this entry needed some definition and a feeling of welcome. Large brick paving pad, overlaid with slate tile porch, intersects driveway's blacktop to spotlight entrance. Arching shadblow trees are informally espaliered against house façade; ground cover is ivy, low-growing yews. Design: Frits Loonsten.

Containers set the tone on sunny streetside entry patio

Because entry had best exposure (southwest), it was enclosed as main outdoor living area.
Left: *Guests enter through door in fence, descend steps to patio, house. Pots of petunias front permanent plants: star jasmine, rhododendron, bird of paradise.* **Right:** *Islands of containers set on basketweave brick paving define seating areas, path to front door. Container plants change with seasons: primroses, florists' cyclamen bloom from fall to spring, followed by pelargoniums, petunias, marigolds. Design: Lawrence Halprin.*

Terraced walls tame a steep hillside

To control slope, design called for system of brick steps **(left),** *retaining walls to lead people up steep hill to entry deck. Design holds slope in place, prevents water runoff. Fence, gate at top of steps gives privacy.* **Right:** *Deck projects 16 feet over slope. Trees, plants on bank give woodsy atmosphere; container plants add touch of color to deck. Structural design: Morris Skenderian. Garden design: Eric Stodder.*

...Entry Gardens

the world watching and still maintain an inviting entryway. The path from street to door should skirt the patio area and be well-defined.

The best way to achieve privacy is to enclose the patio area with a fence, garden wall, or dense hedge. Screens and baffles can also create privacy. Courtyards are intriguing—people like to imagine what's inside. For maximum privacy, you'll want a screen at least 5 to 6 feet tall.

If you like the idea of enclosing the entry area with a high wall, you should check with your local building code to see what the restrictions are. Many areas limit the height of fences and walls and also regulate setbacks and fence placements.

Entryway lends room for private patio space

Portion of entry (top) next to busy intersection was enclosed by wooden fence to form a private patio. (Local ordinances allowed this front area to be fenced.) Fence is 1 by 1s spaced ½ inch apart vertically on both sides of fence; posts are 2 by 6s. Floor surface is exposed aggregate concrete paving sections separated by wooden header boards. Sections of paving were removed to create planting islands; mugho pine, sedum fill bed in foreground. Nandina growing against fence, plant islands soften strong structural lines of house, fence. Seasonal annuals grow in beds along fence; containers of flowers, bird of paradise, succulents complete the landscape. **Below:** *Entry, separated from patio by fence, has spacious, 9-foot-wide entry walk of exposed aggregate paving. Large containers of podocarpus line garage wall, driveway. Area in front of fence facing street is planted with bold agave, ivy ground cover for low maintenance. Fence around new patio partitions outdoor living space, helps define house entry. Design: Gil Rovianek.*

New brick wall made all the difference

Opening through 8-foot brick wall (top) leads to private, tree-roofed patio by front door. Wall, enclosing area between house wings, is painted to match siding. **Below:** *Door in brick wall opens to small (6 by 12 feet) wooden entry deck, constructed of 2 by 4s laid on top of old concrete walk. Design: Jack Chandler.*

19 Popular Ground Covers

Ground covers provide the unifying element in most mini-landscapes. They can substitute for a conventional patch of lawn or serve as the base for the other permanent plantings. Ground covers also hide clutter—debris from falling leaves or flowers, dying annuals or fading bulbs—or barren spots in the garden.

Unless otherwise noted in the individual plant description, the ground covers listed below are easy to find. Your local nursery or garden center will carry the variety of each plant that grows best in your climate. Be sure to specify that you want the low growing, creeping, or spreading form.

Ajuga. Dark green or purplish green leaves that form a thick carpet; blue flower spikes in spring, early summer. Grows rapidly; hardy to 3°F.

Baby's tears. Tiny round leaves form a lush green mat. Rapid grower; best in partial or full shade. Freezes to a black mush in hard frosts, but comes back fast.

Campanula. Heart-shaped, toothed green leaves with star-shaped, lavender blue or white flowers in spring, early summer. Hardy in sub-zero weather. Grows rapidly in partial to full shade.

Euonymus. Rich, dark green leaves with toothed edges. Rapid grower. Tolerates sun or shade; likes good soil and normal watering. Hardy in sub-zero weather. Be sure to get creeping form.

Honeysuckle. Deep green, oval leaves with whitish fragrant flowers in late spring, summer. Rapid grower that can be invasive; hardy in sub-zero weather but may be deciduous. Likes sun; tolerates most conditions.

Hypericum. Medium green leaves in sun, yellow green in shade; bright yellow flowers. Hardy to 0°F.; may be semi-deciduous in cold winter areas. Rapid grower; tolerates poor soils.

Ice plant. Fleshy, succulent leaves; flower color depends on variety. Hardy from 15° to 25°F.; commonly grown in California, Arizona. Will tolerate some drought when established. Give full sun; won't take foot traffic.

Ivy. Leaves come in many shapes and shades of green. Very rapid grower; hard to contain. Some varieties hardy in sub-zero weather. Sun or shade. Probably the most commonly grown ground cover.

Kinnikinnick, Bearberry. Glossy green, persistent leathery leaves that turn red in coldest winters; white or pink flowers, red or pink fruits. Good on steep slopes. Not successful in humid southeast.

Mondo grasses (liriope and ophiopogon). Grasslike clumps that do not spread. Plant closely together for good display. Not recommended for steep slopes. Moderate grower; hardy in sub-zero weather.

Mosses, Scotch and Irish. Not true mosses, but have the same soft, compact, mosslike appearance. Moderately good growers; best in limited areas such as between stepping stones. Hardy in sub-zero weather; likes partial to full sun.

Pachysandra. Dark green foliage with small spikes of fragrant white flowers in summer. Rapid grower; hardy in sub-zero weather. Partial to full shade. Not good on steep slopes.

Periwinkle (Vinca). Dark green, glossy leaves; flowers can be white, wine red, lavender, or blue. Rapid grower; partial to full shade. Hardy in sub-zero weather; tolerates moist, acid soils.

Potentilla. Bright green or gray green leaves; butter yellow flowers in spring, summer. Hardy in sub-zero weather, but may turn brown. Will tolerate moist soils. Ask for creeping form.

Sedum. Succulent leaves with small, star-shaped flowers. Ask for small trailing forms. Rapid grower; hardy from 0° to 15°F. Full sun to partial shade; will tolerate poor soils.

Snow-in-Summer (Cerastium). Silvery gray, woolly leaves in dense tufty mats; masses of snowy white flowers in early summer. Plant in full sun, or light shade. Not as long lived as many ground covers. Hardy in sub-zero weather.

Star jasmine. Glossy, dark green foliage; clusters of white, very fragrant flowers in summer. Slow to start; rapid grower when established. Hardy from 13° to 25°F. in areas without hard frosts.

Strawberry, wild. Small, dark green leaves with white spring flowers. Hardy to 0°F. Common in Pacific Coast states. Partial shade to full sun. Tolerates moist, acid soils. Not grown for edible berries.

Thyme, creeping. Roundish, dark green, aromatic leaves; purplish white, white, red, or pink flowers in summer. For small areas, filler between steppingstones where foot traffic is light. Hardy in sub-zero weather.

...Entry Gardens

All you see from the street is trees and fence

Total privacy enjoyed in street-facing entry courtyard thanks to high wooden fence. Double doors in fence swing open for parties. Loose-laid brick paving has cutouts for informal plant beds, existing trees. Design: W. David Poot.

A narrow-space, leafy retreat

*Since house covered most of 60 by 89-foot lot, front area became both entry and patio. Wooden screen, gate (**top**) keep area private. A 6-foot-high brick wall built along legal setback line encloses patio, adds texture. **Below:** Viewed from second level, plants partially hide 12 by 14-foot deck. Lush plantings of podocarpus, nandina, Oregon grape, ferns on both sides of entry define walk, screen out neighbors, add feeling of space. Two acacia trees outside brick wall block street view, traffic noise. Structural design: Paul W. McKim. Garden design: Todd Fry.*

Borrowed space becomes patio off dining room

Created from front yard area that was once part of entry, private patio opens off dining room, kitchen, is handy for barbecues, outdoor meals. Vertical board fence features kiosklike lights, decorative panels. Tall, pointed-leaf plant is bronze dracaena. Design: Marc Askew.

Mazelike entrance takes you in

*Used brick wall, wrought iron gate (**top**) open into sunny entry courtyard. Since front of house had best sun exposure, designer put main outdoor living space here. Concrete paving is edged with brick to create square pattern; brick edging repeats brick in wall. Plant beds follow shape of wall; green background formed by rhododendrons, azaleas, viburnum, apricot espalier with yellow marigolds, lobelia, trimmed boxwood balls up front. **Right:** Sidewalk entrance leads guests through ivory-colored picket fence, then around brick wall to the left. Gate is hidden behind wall, plants Marigolds, fibrous begonias color up edges of fence, wall. Fence-high rhododendrons provide spring color, complete landscape. Design: W. David Poot.*

…Entry Gardens

Hillside entry devotes entire slope to flowers, shrubs, ground covers; wooden stairs curve up the middle to house. Low, stone retaining walls hold slope in place. Flat stepping-stones, Irish moss cover level area at base of hill. Specimen Japanese maple conceals light at first step; additional lights hidden in foliage at intervals. Mass of color provided by maple's reddish green foliage, annuals, bulbs, ground covers. Alyssum, ferns, other spreading plants hide bulb's spent foliage. Cypress hedge at left screens out neighbors, hides a chain link fence. Design: William Kapranos.

Gravel walk is extension of driveway

For unity in small entry, designer extended gravel driveway up to front door, around circle of lawn, and down side yard. Continuation of single paving material creates expansive feeling. House entry is screened from neighbors, street, by barberry, birches, other dense foliage plants. Pachysandra serves as ground cover; petunias, fibrous begonias lend touch of color. Greenhouse window adds architectural interest, keeps entry green even in snow season. Design: Jerald Kamman.

Restored Victorian evokes the past

Wooden steps lead up to wide, old-fashioned porch for gracious entrances. Pots hold ivy, succulents, nemesia, rose-of-heaven. Rose trained as standard, ivy in tree-shaped topiary add eye appeal. Garden is filled with vintage flowers to add to turn-of-the-century atmosphere. Small gathering of antique bears watches the world go by.

Entry garden puts street a shady distance away

Before this front area was enclosed with a vertical slat fence, the house's full-length windows and sliding glass door (left of photo) directly faced the street. Now, fence and overhead add privacy, wooden decking defines patio area. Gate opens off driveway; path to front door skirts seating area. Plantings of rhododendrons, azaleas soften bare wood of fence, create green backdrop for pots of colorful impatiens, hydrangea. Street tree outside patio area offers shade, more greenery. Pine bonsai, hanging plants complete landscape. Design: Robert W. Chittock.

Stairs off private boardwalk lead to elevated deck

Herringbone-patterned steps gradually guide guests down slope to entertaining deck reached by stairs at rear of house; side yard creates festive outdoor access for parties, also leads to side door off kitchen. Ivy, asparagus ferns spill over top, down face of high, concrete retaining wall at left. More ivy serves as ground cover. Cool, sheltered side yard is perfect for shade-loving plants; rhododendrons, ferns, dogwood, fibrous begonias, impatiens all thrive in dappled sunlight. Design: John Bentley.

Long, Narrow Side Yards

Solutions for the squeeze play

Even the most open-minded gardener sometimes finds that a long, narrow side yard inspires only long, narrow thinking. Most side yards serve as little more than pathways from the street to the rear of the house. They fill up with utility items such as trash cans, tool and firewood storage, and gas and water meters. Many have structures on both sides; house walls, fences, hedges, and retaining walls are common barriers. Light levels vary from full sun to deep shade or alternate between wide extremes—full morning sun with shady afternoons or cool, shaded mornings followed by hot afternoon sun.

Instead of hiding this valuable space behind a fence or screen or simply ignoring it, try giving it a new personality. Forget routine treatments for the walkway and bare-bulb lighting—shape the path to allow for large flower beds and a mini-patio, and use small spot-lights to accent interesting plants or architectural features. Find an out-of-the-way corner to camouflage utilities and storage areas. With just a little innovation, you can turn your side yard into an asset.

I ask not for a larger garden
But for finer seeds.
　　My Prayer. Stanza I, Russell Herman Conwell

Make It More Than a Passageway

Begin your planning with a check list of items your side yard should include. If it's a major path-way from the street to the house entrance or to the back yard, you'll want an attractive, inviting, and safe walk. If it's used after dark, some light-ing will be in order. Determine how much storage space you'll need. If the side yard is your only outdoor area, it should double as a patio or terrace and garden.

Once these essentials are taken care of, you can begin to fill in the spaces with your own individual touches.

To lessen the tunnel effect of a long, narrow en-closed space, make the path meander pleasantly. Doing this also allows for larger areas of plantings and possible space for an outdoor living area. Stairways can curve a bit, too. The shortest dis-tance between two spots is not always the most pleasing.

A good pathway provides a smooth, even surface to lead you from one spot to another. If the walk involves a slope, well-spaced steps should guide you up or down. A gate at either end (or at both ends) adds an interesting structural element and gives the area a feeling of privacy as well.

Since the purpose of a path is to direct people's movement, be sure it is safe. Steps and walks should have smooth, easy-to-walk-on surfaces, such as concrete, exposed aggregate concrete, brick, crushed gravel, wooden decking, or suitable

Prescription for a side yard
To fit outdoor living into very tight space, redwood deck was laid over existing concrete paving. Benches along deck's edge give vertical dimension, making space seem wider. Behind benches: fatsia, evergreen pear. Design: Philip S. Grimes.

The Art of Espaliering

Espaliering—the training of a plant into a definite pattern usually against a flat surface—is an exacting but rewarding art. And it works perfectly in small gardens to create a specimen worthy of a close-up look.

An espalier can be trained in the most confined space against a house wall, fence, screen, or garden wall. The pattern can be an informal one that follows the natural growth habit of the plant or a more formal, symmetrical design.

Most informal espaliers require only pruning of crossing branches or those that don't lie flat. More time is required with symmetrical espaliers in order to plan the design and train the plant.

Almost any tree, shrub, or woody vine with branches flexible enough to train can be espaliered. Fruit trees make especially good subjects because the open design exposes a maximum of branch surface to the sun, stimulating heavier flower and fruit production. For small gardens, choose dwarf varieties of apple, pear, apricot, cherry, or citrus.

In temperate climates reflected heat from a south wall is ideal to help ripen fruit and flowers, but another exposure would be better in hot weather areas.

The steps below show one way to train a fruit tree. Supports should be sturdy enough to hold branches loaded with fruit. Use posts of galvanized pipe or wood (4 by 4-inch) and 14-gauge galvanized wire between supports. Leave 4 to 12 inches between the trellis and wall for free air circulation and for working room.

Other plants that make good espaliers for small-space gardens include camellias (*Camellia japonica* 'Elegans' and *C. sasanqua*), cotoneasters with weeping branches, figs with woody stems, fuchsias with upright growth, podocarpus, pyracantha, sweet olive, viburnum, and vine maple.

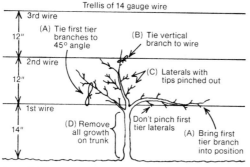

Step 1: First growing season

When vertical resprouts (at angled cut), begin to train 1st tier branches. Tie vertical to 2nd wire. Choose branches for next tier. Pinch tips of rest.

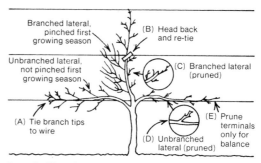

Step 2: First dormant season

Head back vertical below 2nd wire. Leave 2 branches for 2nd tier; cut back others to stubs with 2-3 spurs. Stubs produce fruit along trunk later.

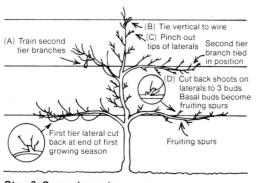

Step 3: Second growing season

Train 2nd tier branches like 1st tier (see step 1). Fruiting spurs will form at base of all laterals below 2nd tier, will produce fruit in a year.

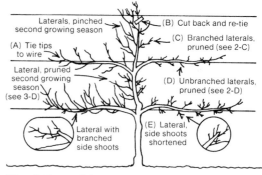

Step 4: Second dormant season

Head back vertical branch below 3rd wire. Prune 2nd tier laterals like 1st tier (see step 2). Continue training in succeeding years, keeping tree to shape.

...Long, Narrow Side Yards

steppingstones or rock slabs. (For more information on walking surfaces, see pages 9-10.) Gear the spacing for stairs and steppingstones to the normal adult walking stride. Landscape architects and engineers recommend a 6-inch rise and at least a 15-inch flat surface as comfortable dimensions for stairs.

If your walk will receive night visitors, adequate lighting is a must. Lights serve two purposes: they illuminate the pathway to safely guide people, and they point out interesting plants or structures and cast unique shadows. (Look for further information on garden lighting on page 11.)

Expand Its Uses

A small patio or terrace area increases the usefulness of a side yard. You will need enough level surface out of the direct traffic pattern to accommodate a bench or small table and chairs. (Choosing garden furniture or built-in seating for small

Railroad tie terracing opens sloping side yard for use

Uphill side yard was converted into multilevel, brick-paved outdoor living area by steps and retaining walls of railroad ties. Raised planting well in center of yard sets traffic pattern, adds visual appeal. Feeling of shelter comes from lush plantings along borders.
Design: Mr. and Mrs. Michael West.

Then a concrete slab, now a cozy eating area

Before, step led from house onto concrete slab. Now, adding floor-level deck and built-in seating made this small space look bigger. Bamboo awning shades new outdoor family mecca. Design: Randall J. Fonce.

Slim, flower-edged deck fills in some dead space

Liability becomes asset when 24-foot-long deck is built in long, very narrow side yard. Surrounded by 5-foot fence, deck becomes private place for child's play, adult's entertaining. Design: Jacque Bowman.

The Versatile Vine

Vines—with their striking foliage or flowers and sometimes colorful fruit—are great concealers. They can hide such eyesores as chain link fences, tree stumps, or drain pipes. They can mask long, blank expanses of fence or house walls. And vines can disguise the fact that small-space gardens have very little growing space to work with.

Some vines, like ivy, attach themselves to almost any surface; others will need some means of support to guide them on their way up. Good supports for vines that climb by twining or tendrils are trellises of wood, wire, or string, and wooden or metal poles or fences.

All the vines listed below are long-lived. Your local nursery or garden center will carry the variety of each plant that grows best in your climate. If you choose a vine for its particular flowers or fruit, be sure to specify which form you want, since some of these plants come from large and varied families.

Akebia. Deciduous twining vine; evergreen in mild climates. Dainty, deep green leaves divided into 3 or 5 leaflets. Inconspicuous dull purple flowers in spring. Plant in sun or shade. Hardy in sub-zero weather.

Bittersweet. Deciduous vine that twines with ropelike branches. Needs support. Light green, toothed foliage; cluster of yellow to orange fruit that split to show red-coated seeds in fall. Ask for fruiting form. Hardy in sub-zero weather.

Boston ivy, Virginia creeper. Closely related deciduous vines valued for quick cover, fall color, hardiness. Will cling to brick, stone, concrete, or wood—or can conceal chain link fence in a hurry. Sun or shade, moderate water and feeding.

Clematis. Deciduous vine; a few are evergreen. Needs support. Attractive flowers in white, pink, reds, purples. Plant deep; keep roots cool. Give lots of water, fertilizer in growing season. Deciduous varieties hardy in sub-zero weather.

Euonymus. Evergreen vine. See page 25.

Fig, creeping. Evergreen vine; attaches firmly to wood, masonry, metal in barnacle fashion. Tiny, heart-shaped, leathery leaves. Keep under control. Turns yellow or will not climb on hot south or west wall. Hardy to 14°F.

Grape. Deciduous; clings by tendrils. American types hardy anywhere, European kinds in the West. In the deep South muscadine grapes are most successful. Can grow very large, but with careful shaping can be kept to reasonable size. Choice for covering arbors or making "eyebrows" on fences. Deep soil, deep planting, careful early training essential to success.

Require annual pruning to control size, insure quality fruit production.

Honeysuckle. Deciduous and evergreen vines. Needs support. (See page 25.)

Hydrangea, climbing. Deciduous vine; has clinging aerial rootlets. Needs support. Heart-shaped leaves; flat, white, lacy flower clusters in summer. Hardy in sub-zero weather.

Ivy. Evergreen vines. (See page 25.)

Jasmine. True jasmines are evergreen or deciduous, have white or yellow flowers. Yellow-flowering kinds tend to be more hardy, less fragrant; the hardiest are deciduous. Not fussy about soil; take sun or part shade. Most are fine-textured, graceful, not too dense.

Passion flower. Fast-growing evergreen or deciduous vines with showy, elaborately constructed flowers in blue, white, pink, or red. Need sun, ample water, occasional thinning out to avoid tangle. Most kinds take light frost; a few tolerate considerable cold. Some bear edible fruits with leathery skins covering juicy pulp.

Potato vine (Solanum). Evergreen vine with white or bright blue flowers. Star-shaped, clustered flowers nearly continuous in mild-winter climates. Not hardy where frosts are severe. Use along fences, posts, arbors. Fast growing but easy to discipline.

Rose (climbers). Deciduous; some may be evergreen in warm winter climates. Needs support. Dark green foliage; flower color, fragrance vary. Needs regular pruning, fertilizer. Buy healthy, disease-resistant plants. Prefers full sun at least half day. Most are hardy in sub-zero weather.

Silver lace vine. Deciduous; hardy to cold, heat, and wind; fast growing; sheeted with white flowers late spring to fall. Easiest care: water once a month, cut back to ground if it grows into a tangle. Takes most soils, heat, sun. May be evergreen in mildest climates.

Star jasmine. Evergreen vine. Not hardy in cold winter areas, but one of the most useful vines where adapted. Glossy foliage; white, fragrant flowers over long spring and summer season. Climbs by twining. Equally useful as ground cover and climbing vine.

Wisteria. Deciduous vine. Needs support. Long flower clusters in purple, white. Not fussy about soil; needs good drainage, ample water during bloom, growth. Keep suckers pulled. Hardy in sub-zero weather.

...Long, Narrow Side Yards

spaces is discussed on page 11.) Screening this area from view with a wall, fence section, or plants will make it even more inviting and private. If the area is in full sun most of the day, you can plant some trees or large shrubs for shade or construct some sort of patio cover. On the other hand, you may want to leave it open for sunning. Plants, furniture, and structures should be kept to a minimum to avoid a crowded appearance.

If the side yard is used to provide storage space for trash cans, firewood, or tools, locate it in an inconspicuous but convenient corner out of the main pathway. You can screen storage from view with a fence, wall, or hedge or dense plantings.

Wooden bridge acts as tree saver
When garden remodeling called for raised grade in side yard, existing goldenrain tree was in trouble. To keep tree at same level, designer put in dry stream bed. "Stream" runs green with hosta, pachysandra, impatiens; bridge over low spot connects gravel walk at tree trunk. Daylilies, petunias, summer annuals fill beds on higher ground. Design: Mark Holeman.

Perking up a humble service area
Steep side yard was terraced with wooden retaining walls to improve basement access; terraces hold ferns, rhododendrons, azaleas. Running bond brick paving covers path, seating area near basement door. Combination bench, planter box filled with petunias, lobelia. Design: Michael Whitmore.

...Long, Narrow Side Yards

Straight and narrow path between two arches
Tiny side yard holds sanctuary at street's edge. Brick wall, step complement pink house walls; arched gate repeats brick arch over statue. Creeping fig, jasmine cover walls; caladium, ferns, grass, boxwood complete garden. Design: Loutrel Briggs.

What About Plants?

Be selective—placing a few really handsome plants in your side yard avoids a crowded or overgrown feeling and gives each plant a chance to shine. Since available light and space will dictate the plants you can consider, choose ones that prefer your particular situation. In full sun, you can plant sun-loving plants or provide some shelter for more tender ones. A long, sunny strip is perfect for a small vegetable patch. For side yards where the light alternates between wide extremes, try using plants in containers that can be moved easily from place to place. To break up stretches of fence or house walls, consider trellised vines or espaliered shrubs and trees. Plants placed in their ideal growing situation will reward you with a maximum of beauty and a minimum of care.

A symmetrical side yard planting pyramid
Precise lines of railroad tie retainers, gravel steps resemble side of pyramid. Even in shade, pachysandra ground cover fills in quickly, holds loose slope in place. Impatiens, variegated hosta add color at base of steps. Design: Mark Holeman.

If you can't fight shade, join it
After years of problems, side yard gave in to shade gardening. Concrete paving blocks meander through trees, shade-loving plants, to rear patio. Gravel mulch keeps watering down, reduces weeds. Design: Frits Loonsten.

Perfect side yard for the fern fancier

With a side yard that offers almost no sun, growing shade-loving plants is the answer. Here, collection of native, other types of ferns grows along house wall in almost constant shade. Ivy, impatiens at far end of bed carry over from front-of-house plantings. (House entrance is pictured on page 28, bottom left.) Gravel path provides secondary route around house. Dense shrubs, birch trees at right screen out neighbors, sun's rays. Design: Jerald Kamman.

A curving path is beguiling

Main house entrance opens into long, narrow yard with a slope, offers double design problem: landscaping needs to make entrance attractive, guide guests to front door, both in narrow, shaded space. Solution? Curving brick steps in basketweave pattern invite people up to brick landing from driveway. Landing has built-in benches for conversation, reading; then steps continue up to brick porch, front door. Retaining walls at end of yard tame slope. Existing trees, some large shrubs were retained to block view of neighbors, reduce street noise. Ground bark mulch keeps plants moist, discourages weeds; bark's reddish color fits with brick, green plants. Design: William Kapranos.

Outdoor Rooms

Atriums, back yards, decks, balconies, rooftops

Skylit garden room is congenial setting for plants

With glass walls, sliding doors on three sides, top open to sky, atrium creates greenhouse atmosphere for plants, family dining. Landscape's focal point is copper beech tree with coppery green foliage, striking shape. In winter, bare branches are strung with twinkle lights; reflections multiply against glass walls for nighttime drama. Other plants include ferns, impatiens, mahonia; house plants, pots of seasonal color occasionally dropped in. Brick floor has drain, can be hosed down to raise humidity level, clean paving. Design: Philip S. Grimes.

Almost everyone would like to increase his living space. And many people with small gardens have found that creating an outdoor room within their garden limits will do just that. No matter where your small-space garden is located—in a back yard, entryway, side yard, or atrium; on a balcony, a deck, or a rooftop—you can change it into the equivalent of an extra room that offers exceptional versatility.

If your outdoor room is to serve as an extension of your interior space, it should reflect the same feeling and style you've created indoors. Repeating materials and color schemes helps connect the two spaces. Try to plan for all the activities you expect the outdoor room to accommodate, such as entertaining, family meals, children's play, sunbathing, reading, or meditating. You should provide furniture for lounging or dining, lights for nighttime use, and plants—both in the garden and as accents in containers—to complete the outdoor feeling.

Good things come in small packages.
  Anonymous

Dealing with Small Spaces

Most people who live on tiny lots already know where their outdoor room will be located—wherever they have the most available space. Builders and developers frequently leave space for an outdoor area at the rear of a house. Though generally hidden from the street, this space often faces several other back yards, alleys, garages, or utility areas filled with trash cans or power poles. Creating privacy will be the first priority.

A good way to make your outdoor room private is to totally enclose it. Solid fences or walls from 5 to 6 feet high will be most efficient; screens, offset sections of fence or wall, a tall hedge, or a bank of fairly dense trees also provide seclusion. Before you enclose your outdoor area, be sure to check local building codes for setback and height restrictions. A building permit may also be needed.

Designers and contractors tend to place the patio or terrace next to the house for easy access and some protection from inclement weather. This placement also gives you an existing wall or two to anchor wind screens and a patio roof. In order to function as living space, the outdoor room may need a floor, furniture, lights, and accessories such as storage areas or a barbecue. The section on general landscaping principles, pages 6-11, deals with the various structural elements you will want to include in your outdoor room.

Suspended Outdoor Space

Balconies and decks, especially those projected out over hillsides, provide for outdoor living and garden space where none existed before. They also share a common feature—both are suspended above the ground, even if only a few inches. Most

Flower color sits near eye level along house's catwalk
Young marigolds and strands of ivy grow in clay pots set in holes of narrow deck's railing. Rail is canted out from deck at 15° angle to allow containers to drain onto ground.

...Outdoor Rooms

are constructed from wooden decking or reinforced concrete slabs. And, as they create a new surface, little grading or leveling of the existing lot will be necessary.

Wind and weight can be troublemakers. Strong winds play havoc with both people and plants, especially on high balconies or exposed decks. The house itself forms the best windbreak. Screens, fences, garden walls, trees, or tall hedges also will be effective.

Garage roof becomes spacious outdoor room
Left: *View of garagetop garden from street.* **Below:** *Closeup of trellis-sheltered rooftop garden. Food is prepared on tiled counter with electrical outlets; 26 feet of built-in seating eliminates need for most outdoor furniture. Planter troughs form walls on all sides of floor decking, can display plants in containers. Others hang from overhead. Storage cabinets are set in under planter trough. Design: John Mason Caldwell.*

Canalside gardening in double row of planter boxes

No tubs or pots for these canalside dwellers. Instead, they opted for grander-scale containers: six 4 by 6-foot planting boxes to edge the deck. Low-growing succulents, conifers keep view of passing boats open. Design: Michael Siegel.

Here's how to make raw decking more inviting

Deck built into rear yard offers welcome outdoor living space. Alternate direction of deck boards adds interest. Plants in pots, brick planter, low beds soften deck edge. Design: William Kapranos.

Weight presents another problem for gardens in the air. Decks and balconies cannot always safely support heavy weights. Plants in raised beds or large containers weigh a great deal, and watering makes them even heavier. People and garden furniture will also add to the total weight. Check the weight limits of your structure with the contractor or builder. If you're renting or leasing, ask the owner or landlord for some guidelines before you begin landscaping.

Most gardening on decks and balconies relies on container plants. Plants grown in pots need more frequent individual attention than those grown in a regular garden, but container gardening also gives you more flexibility. Plants past their prime can easily be replaced, and, on a whim, you can rearrange the containers to create a different look. Special techniques for container gardening are offered on pages 56-57.

A few decks that rest just inches above the ground level cut out areas of decking to incorporate existing plants into the landscape. Container plants will serve as accents.

When Your House Contains an Atrium

The atrium—an interior garden room enclosed by house walls and open to the sky—requires some special gardening know-how. Most atriums have two or more walls of glass that create garden views and increase light levels and the feeling of space and airiness for the adjoining rooms. Atriums also modify the normal climate, sheltering the garden from such weather extremes as prevailing winds and severe temperatures. They may be sun traps, a plus during cold winters but a possible problem in hot weather.

Since your atrium will be on view constantly, it should always look its best. Try to use plants that perform well throughout the year with a minimum of care. Slow-growing evergreens make good choices for ground covers and background shrubs or small trees. You can add seasonal color with annuals in pots. Unlike most gardens, an atrium is visually limited by the interior spaces that enclose it, so plants and garden furniture should be kept in scale with the atrium's dimensions.

(Continued on page 46)

17 Garden Trees to Consider

Trees have always been the backbone of most landscape designs. In the small-space garden, though, the ultimate size a tree will reach, both in height and spread, limits your choices. Because of this, the following list of suggested trees includes only a few that will grow taller than 35 feet.

Keep in mind the amount of care and maintenance a tree may require. Trees that are grown for their flowers and fruit, both decorative and edible, always produce seasonal litter. Even though deciduous trees lose their leaves annually, the fact that they let more light into the house and garden during winter months is a decided "plus."

Since a tree dominates all other plant types, especially in a small-space garden, most landscape designs should include only one or two. Many of the trees listed produce several spectacular effects: flowers, fruit, fall color, and interesting winter branch structures.

Because some of these trees are regional favorites, ask your nurseryman for his opinion on the right tree for your garden. Be sure to ask for the variety that only reaches about 35 feet in height at maturity—some of these trees have very tall relatives.

Birch. Deciduous. May grow quite tall (over 35 feet) rapidly, but never appears massive. Usually planted in groups. Decorative bark in white, tan, pinkish brown peels in layers. May be susceptible to certain pests and diseases.

Citrus. Evergreen. Dwarf varieties best in small spaces. Grow slowly to about 10 feet. Lemon, lime, and grapefruit are most common. Only for mild winter areas.

Corkscrew willow. Deciduous. Grows fast to 30 feet tall. Needs less water than most willows. Leaves are twisted and curled into rings or circles. Has dramatic winter branch pattern.

Crabapple, flowering. Deciduous. Moderate growth rate to 25 feet tall. Grown for masses of spring bloom; some produce decorative fruit.

Dogwood. Deciduous. Slow growing to about 20 feet. Grown for profuse white or pink spring bloom; some varieties have fall leaf color. Hardy to 0°F. Cornelian cherry variety has small, inconspicuous yellow flowers; showy, edible, scarlet fruits. Withstands sub-zero weather; one of the earliest dogwoods to bloom.

Goldenchain tree. *(Laburnum)* Deciduous. Fast growing to 30 feet tall. Grown for spectacular display of yellow, wisterialike blossoms. All parts of this tree are poisonous. Remove seed pods; they can drain the tree's strength. Can be trained as single or multitrunked plant.

Goldenrain. Deciduous. Slow to moderate growth to 35 feet. Emerging spring leaves are salmon colored. Large clusters of yellow summer flowers are followed by tawny, lantern-like fruit.

Hawthorn. Deciduous. Moderate growth rate to 25 feet. Angular branching with a tendency to grow multiple trunks with rough bark. Blooms in late spring, followed by tiny fruit. Red fall color.

Japanese maple. Deciduous. Slow growing to 20 feet tall and as wide. Graceful, delicate foliage and branch pattern. Spring and fall foliage color.

Magnolia. Deciduous. Grow the small varieties. Delicate, waxy, fragrant spring bloom, interesting seed pods. Dark green, sometimes glossy foliage. Flowers can be damaged in late frosts.

Olive, European. Evergreen. Slow growing to 30 feet tall. Hardy to 20°F. Gray green foliage. Needs full sun. Can be trained as single or multi-trunked. Fruit is attractive but messy. Plant fruitless varieties or spray to avoid fruit setting.

Pear, ornamental. Deciduous or evergreen. Moderate growth to 25 feet tall. White flower clusters in spring; small, inedible fruit; wine red to scarlet fall color on deciduous varieties. Can be grown as a single or multitrunked tree, or espaliered.

Pine. Evergreen. Choose small varieties that only reach about 25 feet tall. Needled leaves in many shades of green. Prefer full sun. Can be shaped or controlled with pruning. Hardiness depends on variety.

Redbud. Deciduous. Fast growing to 35 feet tall. Dark brown bark. Several flower colors in spring. Fall foliage color. Decorative seed pods during winter.

Shadblow, Service berry. Deciduous. Slow growing to 30 feet tall. Delicate, often multi-trunked. Produces spring flowers, summer edible fruit, glowing autumn color, and good winter branch pattern. Casts light shade. Roots aren't invasive. Needs cold winter.

Silk tree. Deciduous. Fast growing to 40 feet tall. Hardy to 0°F, likes summer heat. Feathery, fernlike, light green foliage. Fluffy pink or red flowers in summer. Tree has spreading, umbrella shape. Casts light shade.

Vine maple. Deciduous. Slow to moderate growth to 35 feet. Delicate, irregular structure; yellow and red blazing fall color. Best in cold climates with some humidity, acid soil. Select in fall to get best forms for autumn color.

...Outdoor Rooms

View balcony shades, forms roof over lower terrace

Cantilevered balcony with wood, steel rod railing, running bond brick paving offers outdoor dining space, panoramic river view. Lower brick terrace is private seating area. Both areas rely on potted plants for seasonal color, native trees, shrubs for foliage. Design: Francis Jones Poetker.

Tightly packed planter boxes decorate small deck

Open air deck provides only level space on steep lot, includes entertaining area, raised planter boxes. Planters edged by neat boxwood contain mass of marigolds, daisies, lobelia. Same flowers fill large clay pots. Existing trees lower on slope add leafy screen. Design: W. David Poot.

Low-level deck designed around existing plants

Small, tree-filled back yard (top) lacked room for outdoor living. To create level area, wooden deck sits about 3 feet off ground, fits into existing trees, shrubs. Left: Deck curves around big boulder. Maples, ferns, rhododendrons, other northwest natives give woodsy feel. Bark mulch keeps soil moist, weed-free. Design: John Herbst, Jr.

Instead of One Large Garden, Five Tiny Ones

The photographs on these pages show how five intimate gardens resulted from a landscape architect's ingenious division of some very awkward space. The house sits only a few feet from the street and takes up almost the entire width of the lot. Rather than hiding or ignoring the often narrow peripheral space, it was split into small areas, each designed for specific uses.

Double gates and fencing hide the entry garden from the street and parking area. The wide pad and steps of aggregate concrete paving offer a visual invitation. Containers on stair steps point guests to the door. The paving extends further to the right, creating space for a small table and chairs.

The fact that the private dining patio backs up to the street is cleverly concealed by the walls of lattice and translucent glass panes. Brick flooring and white latticework screens lend a European feeling to the area. Offset screens hide the utility areas located on either side but leave them open for easy access. Forming the backbone of this garden are container plants that can be rotated with the seasons.

Sun floods the wooden deck off the bathroom, creating a perfect spot for sunbathing and growing succulents in containers. A high wooden fence assures total privacy.

The serene garden off the master bedroom offers a cool restful spot for reading, meditation, or just daydreaming. The cement steps were designed to be wide enough to accommodate cushions for seating. This garden also provides a pleasant view from the bedroom and hall. The path beyond the screen leads to the dining patio.

Located off the house dining room and near the kichen is the fifth small space, a loggia—an open, roofed gallery common in Italy. It increases room for entertaining by providing table and chairs for outdoor meals and a seating area for private conversations. The glass wall at the end of the loggia protects occupants from prevailing winds. Because it is sheltered, this area houses a collection of exotic plants requiring tender care.

Plants in containers serve as the garden in these small spaces; permanent plantings form a green backdrop. Since these close-to-the-house compact areas are always on view, plants should look their best at all times. Plants in containers can be replaced easily when flowers or foliage pass their prime.

Design: Roy Rydell.

Containers point the way to handsome front door
Double gates open into small entryway. Exposed aggregate concrete paving with wooden header boards reflects light, heat; good for sun-loving citrus, succulents in pots.

For outdoor dining, an airy loggia adjoins garden
Corner wind screen of full-length windows at far end of open loggia controls wind, still lets in light. Tender plants thrive in sheltered alcove.

Burst of white latticework encloses diminutive dining nook
Windowed wooden screen, latticework panels make area intimate, protect from wind, hot sun.

Haven for sun worshippers: tiny deck off bathroom
Surrounded by high fence on three sides, pocket deck traps heat, sunlight, is perfect for private sunbathing. Plants in landscape also thrive in heat: citrus, succulents, bamboo, flowering annuals. Steps lead down into mini-garden.

Off-bedroom patio sets tranquil mood
Secluded, shady patio creates restful view for bedroom, good spot for reading, thinking, other quiet pursuits. Wide steps can hold cushions for seating, double as plant platforms. All-green plantings contrast well with terra cotta background color of house exterior.

Atrium surrounded by house is leafy enclave

Steppingstone path winds from glass door in entry through atrium to sliding glass doors of den. Atrium creates garden views for rooms on all sides. Birch trees, natural stone sculpture are focal points; evergreen shrubs, bergenia, ground covers of ivy, vinca fill out landscape. Ivy on wall at left conceals brick chimney. Design: Shurcliff & Merrill.

...Outdoor Rooms

Choosing plants that will grow in your atrium can be an art. Before you plan the landscape, you should study how much light and heat it traps. If your atrium has low light levels, you may need to use plants that thrive in shady spaces. Because it's enclosed by house walls, it gives tender plants some protection from frost. Above all, you will want plants that need very little maintenance.

If trapped sun will be a problem during warm weather, you can provide shade for both plants and people with overhead screens or roofing sections. You can create some air circulation by opening a door or window to let in cool air at a low level; warm air will rise and escape through the roof opening. A deciduous shade tree can help solve the problem by providing cool shade in the summer and by letting the winter sun shine through the bare branches to warm the atrium.

River birch dominates atrium near entry

Atrium garden imitates nearby woods with pebble-lined, dry stream bed; large, natural stones seemingly placed at random; mixture of tiny rocks, ground bark covering ground. Even falling leaves, other normal litter seems to fit into design. River birch, ferns, evergreens, other plants are native to local area. Design: Richard Gale.

Explosion of greenery in atrium at house's core

Densely planted atrium fills glass walls with green foliage. Pots of red geraniums create spot of color now; seasonal flowers will replace them later. Basketweave paving can be watered down to cool area off. Add portable furniture for pleasant patio living. Design: Robert C. Marvin.

Hold That Hill with Retaining Walls

When much of your small space sits on a hillside or slope, a retaining wall can increase your usable outdoor living space.

If you have less than a 36 percent slope and your retaining wall will be no more than 2 or 3 feet tall, you can build it yourself. But if you're planning a taller wall or one on a steeper slope, contact a landscape architect or contractor for advice; then get bids from general or landscape contractors for the actual construction.

If you have tricky soil such as marsh land, adobe, or fill—or if your area could experience an earthquake or landslide—you should call in an engineer. Oozing mud caused by improper drainage could also create problems. A retaining wall that collapses or fails to hold the slope in place could cause serious damage to your home or a neighbor's home downhill.

Providing drainage for retaining walls

Proper drainage of both surface and subsurface water will be crucial. Ditches, gutters, drain tiles, and proper plantings can be combined to divert excess surface water from rain or irrigation.

As soil becomes saturated, excess water accumulates below the surface and flows downhill. When subsurface water reaches an obstruction, it collects, building up pressure that may burst or undermine the wall. Subsurface water should be collected in gravel backfill and directed around the edge of the wall via drain pipes or tiles or allowed to escape through weep holes in the wall. A special surface gutter for water from weep holes prevents the water from pouring over the lawn or patio.

Any hillside drainage system should funnel toward a storm sewer, ditch, or natural drainage.

What a wall is made of

In a small garden where everything is visible, you should choose the building materials carefully. The following list contains those most commonly used:

Concrete. Three types of concrete are suitable for retaining walls: concrete cast in place in preconstructed forms; mortared concrete building blocks with steel reinforcement anchored in a solid cast concrete foundation; and slump block (hollow concrete block that looks like adobe) with vertical steel reinforcing rods embedded in a concrete foundation. Of the three, cast concrete is the strongest.

Clay bricks. Bricks can be used for low walls and raised beds.

Natural stone. For very low walls and raised beds, stones can be laid dry—their uneven surfaces hold them in place. You can grow plants between the stones to increase soil retention. For higher walls, set stones in mortar and provide a poured concrete foundation.

Wood. Properly treated wood, secured by supports anchored in soil or concrete, provides a strong, long-lasting wall. Walls built with 2 by 6 or 10-inch boards with 4 by 4-inch support posts should be limited to 2 or 3 feet in height.

Plants for retaining walls

Planting a retaining wall serves two purposes: plant roots help hold soil in place, and foliage helps conceal and enhance the wall surface, providing elevated (and perhaps vertical) color. You should choose hardy, firm-rooted plants like English ivy or trailing juniper that cover well.

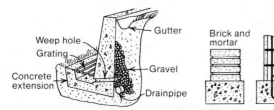

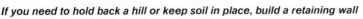

If you need to hold back a hill or keep soil in place, build a retaining wall

From left to right: Cross section of masonry wall shows ways of draining excess water. Low masonry walls need concrete footing slightly wider than walls; set steel reinforcement for hollow concrete blocks in footing. Wooden wall is 4 by 4s, planks; posts braced into hill. Stack large rocks directly on slope; plants, root systems hold rocks in place.

...Outdoor Rooms

Carport wall adds flair to small garden

Below: Shingled carport wall creates nooks for shrubs; overhanging beam ends form trellises for grape vines. Grapestake fencing is used beside gate, elsewhere in yard.
Left: Wider view of rear yard shows two focal points— large wooden deck and hexagonal gazebo—widely separated across lawn for feeling of depth and openness. Staggered, four-stall carport at right was shingled to match mansardlike gazebo roof. From garden side, carport wall is edged to serve as backdrop for planting beds. Container plants on deck add to garden's lush look. Design: Owen Peters.

In Lilliput space, people, dog, plants flourish

Right: Garden only 18 feet deep, 32 feet wide suits family. There's space for outdoor living in sun or shade, a place for child and dog to play, and still room for a 45-square-foot vegetable garden. Hanging baskets increase planting space in outdoor room. Trellis of ½ by 2s spaced 4 inches apart spans paving from house to storage shed. **Top:** View from den shows outdoor dining area. Trellis shades table, shields glass wall of den. Design: Michael Byrne.

Good things happen to an awkward triangle

*Odd-shaped triangular space used for off-street guest parking sat between house and alley. It left house exposed to wind, dust, public view. Owners' solution was to fill space with an open-air lath structure combining guest parking, outdoor garden room, attractive house entrance. **Right:** View from alley shows guest carport, back of lath structure.*
Bottom right: *Garden room built of 8-foot-high cedar screens of 2 by 4s and 1 by 1-inch lath has built-in benches, garden pool. Overhead uses heavier lumber for stability, strong shade pattern. Potted plants, hanging baskets provide green relief.* ***Bottom left:*** *Garden pool makes use of vintage bathtub that sits in frame of 2 by 4s; deck is 18 inches off ground. Concealed pump recirculates water through lava rock, potted foliage plants, with a musical trickle. Nighttime lighting adds a touch of magic.*

Water and the Small Garden

Nothing lends a feeling of serenity to a garden like a gurgling fountain or a decorative pool of shimmering water. But in a small-space garden, even a tiny pool or fountain becomes a major focal point. For this reason, size and scale are important. The pool should be kept small and planted simply to assure that everything will be in proportion.

Garden supply stores or statuary shops often carry tiny, easy-to-install pools. Some are simple bowls of metal or poured concrete; others come with fountains, spouting jets of water, or two- or three-tiered spill trays that may or may not require a recirculation system. If your design calls for something more elaborate, you should consult an architect, landscape architect, or pool specialist (look in the yellow pages of your local telephone book under Fountains, Water Gardens, etc.).

Many plants will grow in or around the outside edge of your garden pool. For plants to grow in soil around the pool's edge, choose some of the many varieties of bog plants that thrive in constantly moist soil. These include papyrus, umbrella plant, horsetail, water iris, ferns, and bamboo. Some plants that will grow in the water itself are water lilies, water hyacinth, water lettuce, eel grass, and lotus.

In handkerchief garden: pool, steppingstones, tree screen
Seen from master bedroom, delightful small garden features concrete pool from 6-18 inches deep. Handsome rocks and plants edge shoreline. In Japanese manner, views beyond garden are screened with pines, maples. Garden fits in space 12 feet wide by 21 feet long. Design: Hoichi Kurisu.

Carport walled off, fountain added to make this entryway a continuing pleasure
Small entry courtyard replaces open carport; three-tier wall fountain contributes water sounds. Plants grow in beds, water box, atop wall. Design: Jongejan and Garrard.

Reflecting pond at garden's edge spanned by small bridge
Serene pool of cast concrete captures mirror image of Japanese maples. Design: Art Mehas.

Glass balls float in cast concrete container
Shady garden addition: miniature pool in container resting on bed of river rocks. Pots of tiger lilies, horsetail add color. Design: Doug Baylis.

In offset pool by entry, water iris grow
Bonsai in concrete container, steppingstones leading over water to dining room ledge, pond filled with koi, water plants give entry oriental flavor. Design: John Herbst, Jr.

Multitrunked olive tree, adobe wall—desert naturals

Gardening in southwest can take on different perspective: sparse landscapes echo nearby desert; plants have subtle colors; buildings, fences, garden walls painted white, beige, other light tone to reflect sun, heat. In this typical courtyard: olive in circular bed, hand-crafted Mexican brick paving, adobe wall with peek-through gate. Container plants at left offer changeable color. Design: Bill Tull.

…Outdoor Rooms

Pocket garden fits between back door and tree

Steppingstones set in grass pave floor of tiny back patio just off back door; area is handy to kitchen, family room for entertaining overflow. Tree trunk serves as bracket base for hanging baskets of impatiens, ivy geranium, summering house plants. Half barrels filled with impatiens sit at tree base. Design: Jerald Kamman.

Stone terrace suggests elegant simplicity

Color comes in containers by seasons to blue stone terrace off back door; here, petunias, begonias bloom. Dogwood gives spring flowers, summer shade. Design: Richard Gale.

Two walled gardens—one compact, one generous
All outdoor space in this house was walled-in for privacy.
Left: *Narrow seating area off dining room with marigolds,*
daisies, shrubs. ***Above:*** *Larger patio off bedroom contains*
garden pool, projects a formal air. Design: W. David Poot.

An entertainment area enframed by shrubs
Traditional city garden uses shrubs, hedges, plants to define space. Design: Thomas Church.

The Small-Space Farmer

You can make space in even the tiniest yard for growing vegetables—in narrow beds, containers, or mixed with flowers in planting beds. Vegetables with brightly colored fruit—peppers and tomatoes, for example—can be used as ornamentals. Leafy vegetables like Swiss chard or leaf lettuce blend well with other plants and will continue to grow if you only harvest the outer leaves. Such fast-growing vegetables as radishes and beets will also make sense in a small garden; you can harvest several crops in a single season. For maximum satisfaction, grow vegetables that you and your family like to eat.

The following list suggests vegetables that adapt well to confinement, either in narrow beds or containers. Most require at least six hours of full sun a day.

Beans. Plant bush or pole varieties.

Beets. Harvest several crops during season.

Carrots. Sow seeds every 2 weeks for continuous harvest. Short varieties adapt to containers.

Chard. The red-stemmed variety, 'Rhubarb', is decorative.

Cucumbers. Plant compact varieties like 'Little Minnie', 'Patio Pik', or 'Tiny Dill'.

Eggplant. Plants and fruit are ornamental.

Endive. Use curly-leafed type as border.

Herbs. Most grow well in containers.

Lettuce. Grow leaf lettuce or the tiny form, 'Tom Thumb'.

Onions. Grow green onions or scallions.

Peppers. Compact plants bear decorative fruit.

Radishes. Plant seeds every few weeks during cool weather for continuous harvest.

Spinach. Harvest outer leaves for continuous harvest.

Tomatoes. Grow all varieties in containers or planting beds.

Vegetables fit neatly into small spaces
*Productive vegetable patch fits in sunny side yard, service area (**top**). Tightly packed lettuce, corn, artichokes share ground space; cucumbers, beans climb up wire hardware cloth trellis. Cherry tomatoes grow in hanging baskets. Sun bounces off white house wall; cast concrete slabs also reflect heat to aid garden. **Right:** Half barrels contain squash, lettuce, standard tomatoes. Barrels provide enough soil space; exposed aggregate concrete paving absorbs heat, reflects light. Design: R. David Adams.*

...Outdoor Rooms

Strong design feature gives an atrium lasting appeal

The best landscaped atriums don't rely completely on plants. To keep them presentable despite plant setbacks, include a strong design feature. In this inside garden off the kitchen, modular decking covers 11 by 14-foot floor.

Wood deck, fish pool combine in unusual atrium garden

A small wood deck at floor grade, fish pool edged with rocks, plants, fill 10 by 10-foot atrium. Two atrium walls are higher than two stories, two are windowless. Birch clump in corner will screen high walls. Design: Ken Wood.

This screened atrium is a 17-foot-wide, 40-foot-long family relaxing center

This house's main outdoor living and gardening area is a completely screened central atrium. Silver gray fiberglass mesh cuts sun, blocks wind and insects. Design: Don Chapman.

The How-to's of Container Gardening

Gardening in containers gives small-space gardeners—even those limited to raising plants in a window box or a tiny balcony—the freedom and flexibility usually associated with much larger gardens. Almost any plant you choose will adapt to a container, at least for a time. You can change flowers with each season and grow trees and shrubs for their interesting shapes, flowers and fruit, or foliage. You can even try vegetables.

Plants that are tender or temperamental in your climate will probably grow in containers because you can place them in a favored location and give them the special care they require. Versatility is also a strong point of containers. They can be quickly rearranged to create a totally new look in your small space.

Once you learn the basics, gardening in containers will be easy. Since the plants are confined, you can give each one individual attention. The following sections contain fundamental information on choosing containers, soil mixes, how to pot plants, and fertilizing and watering techniques.

Choosing containers. Clay pots, wooden boxes, half-barrels, baskets—anything that holds enough soil to support a plant can be a container. When you purchase a container, look for a style and material that complements the rest of your landscape and the style of your home. Containers in small spaces become an integral part of the design. Check to be sure the container you select has a drainage hole. If not, you'll need to provide a drainage layer to catch excess water.

Red clay pots, always popular, are porous, allowing them to absorb moisture and permit air circulation. Though it's difficult to overwater plants growing in clay pots, these containers can be quite heavy when planted.

Especially suitable for use indoors or on patios, glazed clay pots have a nonporous finish that prevents moisture loss and cuts water use.

Good wooden containers should be decay-resistant and thick enough to prevent the hot summer sun from drying out soil and roots too quickly. Durable woods, such as redwood, oak, and cedar, are widely used for containers.

How to water. Constant exposure to drying air on all sides makes plants grown in containers dry out much faster than plants in open ground. Add to this the differences in seasons, plant species, container types and sizes, and locations and it's difficult to know exactly when to water.

A good method is to inspect the top inch of the potting mix with your finger. If the soil feels dry to the touch, water the plant. You'll soon get to know the individual needs of your container plants.

On hot or windy days you may need to water more often. In cool, damp weather and during their dormant season, plants will need water less frequently.

Apply water directly into the top of the container, allowing any excess to run freely from the drainage hole for at least a minute. To water containers without a drainage hole, add enough water to equal about one quarter the total soil volume. This amount should be adequate for the plant's needs without drowning it.

A gentle flow from a hose with a spray attachment or a watering can with a sprinkler nozzle is probably the easiest way to water. Severe blasts of water from a hose can gouge out holes in the soil, exposing plant roots.

Another method is to water plants from below by placing them in a large trough or container partially filled with water for 20 or 30 minutes. Or you can submerge pots in larger containers of water and wait until the bubbles stop.

When you go on vacation, ask a friend to follow your instructions on when and how much to water your plants. As an alternative, you can place pots in a shallow trench filled with wet sawdust or peat moss. Indoor plants will absorb moisture easily when placed on ½ to 2-inch-thick bricks in a tub or sink filled with water halfway up the side of the bricks.

Soil mixes for container gardening. Good potting soil combines organic materials (ground bark, peat moss, sawdust, leaf mold) and mineral materials (sand, vermiculite, perlite) to create a mix that will drain freely, provide ample air for roots, and supply enough nutrients for good plant growth. You can buy packaged container mix from a nursery or garden center or make your own mix.

To make a good basic mix, combine 2 cubic feet of nitrogen-stabilized ground bark, peat moss or other organic material; 1 cubic foot of sharp sand (not ocean sand) or sandy loam; 1⅓ cups 0-10-10 dry fertilizer (for more information on fertilizer, see page 13); and 1¾ cups dolomite limestone. This will yield about 3 cubic feet of container mix.

Indoor containers, hanging baskets, and containers for balconies or decks will need a lightweight mix. Blend 2 parts of the basic mix (see above) with 1 part vermiculite or perlite.

Azaleas, rhododendrons, camellias, and fuchsias prefer a slightly acid soil mix. Check with your local nursery or garden center; they should carry a packaged acidic soil mix.

Because these mixes contain no nitrogen, they can be stored as long as 6 months in a dry spot. You will need to add nitrogen fertilizer—in slow-release capsules, dry or liquid forms—at planting time to insure proper plant growth.

How to pot plants. Before you begin, be sure the container is clean. If the container has been used, scrub it with hot water and a brush to eliminate any pests or soil diseases. Soak a porous pot in water before planting so it won't absorb moisture from the potting mix. Otherwise, the root ball could shrink away from the container's sides, allowing water to drain away without wetting the root ball.

Cover the drainage hole with a curved pot shard, stones, or a square of fine-mesh wire screen to prevent clogging and minimize soil loss. For containers without drainage holes, you can spread a ½ to 1-inch layer of coarse sand or small pebbles mixed with granulated gardening charcoal in the bottom. This layer acts as a reservoir to catch any excess moisture.

Wet the soil of each plant before removing it from its nursery container to keep the root ball intact. To remove a plant from a small pot, invert the pot with one hand, using the other hand to support the root ball; then tap the pot gently against a ledge or solid surface to loosen it.

For a plant in a metal can, use tin snips or a can cutter to cut the sides apart; then turn the container on its side, loosen the root ball, and gently ease it out.

If the plant roots are tightly compacted (a condition known as "rootbound" or "potbound"), score the roots lightly in several places with a sharp knife and loosen them gently with your fingers. For severely potbound plants whose roots have formed a solid mass, make several cuts from top to bottom on the root ball, then run your fingers through the cuts to loosen or fray the roots.

Try this trick for repotting success
Before setting plant in new container, shave root ball, making ¼-inch cuts with sharp knife. Drop into pot (usually one size larger than present one) and fill in edges with new soil.

Once the plant is out of its former container, pour moist—not soggy—potting mix into the new pot. Put in enough mix to bring the top of the root ball to about 1 or 2 inches below the rim. Continue filling in around the root ball with potting mix, tamping it lightly with each addition.

Newly potted plants should be watered thoroughly. To help them withstand the shock of transplanting, set the plants in a shady, protected location for several days.

Fertilizing container plants. Container plants need to be fertilized to replace soil nutrients used up by the plants or leached away by watering.

Liquid fertilizer and slow-release capsules are two popular types used in containers. Watering with a diluted liquid fertilizer is convenient and fast-acting; light applications twice a month should encourage steady growth. With slow-release fertilizer granules or capsules buried in the potting mix, nutrients will gradually diffuse into the soil when moistened. Slow-release fertilizers last varying lengths of time.

You should always read the label directions on fertilizers and carefully follow their instructions. Too much fertilizer can be as harmful as too little.

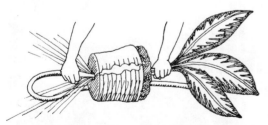

When plant outgrows pot, here are two solutions
Top: Let soil dry slightly to shrink root ball. Then, supporting plant, tap cloth-protected container rim with mallet and slide out. Bottom: Float root ball out by forcing water through drain hole.

Picture Gardens

You can "paint" living pictures with plants

From the inside of your house, you and your guests look out on certain portions of your garden much of the time—those parts that can be seen through windows, glass walls, and glass doors. Although any glimpse of greenery is welcome, the most pleasant garden views result from deliberate planning. Since they will be framed by house walls or a door frame, think of these tiny view gardens as pictures.

People plant vista gardens for several reasons: to create an interesting view from indoors; to gain privacy for rooms that face streets, sidewalks, alleys, or other public areas; or to bring a garden feeling into a room, such as a bathroom or bedroom, while still maintaining its privacy.

Because these small gardens will always be visible, you should choose plants that will be interesting year-round and need a minimum of maintenance.

"Nature will bear the closest inspection. She invites us to lay our eye level on her smallest leaf, and take an insect view of its plain."
    Journals, *22 October 1839, Henry David Thoreau*

Plant a Garden Vista

When you begin planning for your garden view, the size of the window determines the number and size of the plants you can use. Full-depth glass walls or doors are the easiest to design and plan for successfully; you can plant from the ground up. One disadvantage to full-length glass is that a stranger or child could walk right into or even through it unless he is stopped by furniture, an object just inside the glass, or something on the glass itself.

Tiny view gardens for windows with sills several feet off the ground offer more of a challenge. You should use plants that grow as high as the window and develop flowers or foliage at that level.

Remember not to overplant by a window. For a small window, one plant may be sufficient. For larger or wider windows, use just enough plants

Step out of the shower, and you think you're outside
Outdoor garden moves inside when bifolding louvered doors are opened. The 6 by 15-foot-long garden is enclosed by 5-foot solid wood fence. Insect screening rises above fence, covers top. Design: Belt Collins & Assoc. Ltd.

Take a bath with the outdoors in view

Private view garden for bathroom, adjoining bedroom spotlights vine maple; tree has airy spring, summer foliage that turns bright red in autumn; stark winter branches also catch the eye. Ferns, other shade plants complete garden. Door in back wall, entered from house exterior, is used for watering, garden maintenance. Design: John Herbst, Jr.

A small-space study in curves

Retaining wall of brown fieldstone curves into hillside to create shady garden alcove outside living room window. Planting bed, gravel paving repeat curve. Design: Mark Holeman.

...Picture Gardens

to be seen and appreciated but not so many that they will grow together, obscuring the view.

To create a private vista garden off a bedroom or bathroom, you can enclose the area with a fence, wall, screen, or dense hedge.

Since plants in totally enclosed gardens need air circulation, create a section that opens or has louvers to let in fresh air. Frequently these private gardens have low light levels, too. If this is the case in your garden, shade-loving plants may be your best choice.

Choosing Plants for Your Vista Garden

Plants for your vista garden should look presentable at all times and provide some seasonal changes, such as flowers, fruit, or fall color. They should be slow growing and keep their shape without too much care to maintain the garden design.

Living room, dining room share garden vista

Both living and dining rooms open on this small, enclosed garden with deck, decorative pond. Fencing improves view by eliminating neighbors' houses, driveway, street. Design: John Herbst, Jr.

Delicate tree silhouette fills two-story window

House entry, flight of stairs, second-floor landing share window view. Tree, growing at lake's edge, pruned for interesting shape. Wooden planters on deck filled with boxwood, marigolds, daisies, lobelia; flowers change seasonally. Design: W. David Poot.

Visual treat for bedroom: clematis on trellis

Floor-to-ceiling window facing fence needed a view in very narrow space. Clematis climbs vertically; trellis adds design. Panel at trellis top shields light. Design: Roy Rydell.

Window boxes—good things in small packages

When you've got the urge to plant and no yard to call your own, window boxes may be the answer. Filled with red geraniums, these boxes rest on window sill, are painted black to match house trim. Because window boxes can be heavy when planted and watered, provide adequate bracing.

Gardens in Shades of Green

In most gardens, green plants serve as the background for seasonal displays of color provided by flowers, berries, and changing or colorful variegated foliage. But occasionally, an entire garden becomes a study in only the many subtle shades of green.

Green gardens can solve problems. They will thrive in very shaded spots that lack enough sun for flowers or colored foliage. And they require little maintenance, especially if most are evergreen trees and shrubs.

A well-designed green garden combines several shades of green, some contrasts in texture, and a pleasant grouping of plant shapes from ground covers to trees. And many green gardens provide some seasonal changes — deciduous plants lose their leaves, revealing bare branches to contrast with the evergreen plants.

The wide variety offered by the various shades of green may surprise many gardeners. Greens vary from light yellow through apple green, medium green, gray green, blue green, to rich dark green. You can also use plants with green variegation. Combinations include yellow and green, white and green, and two to three varying shades of green on the same leaf.

Texture and plant shape create other points of interest in the green garden. You'll enjoy the contrasts of evergreen needles with broad leaves or smooth, shiny leaves with dull, hairy, or heavily veined leaves. The wide variety of available plant shapes, sizes, and growth habits greatly increases the number of possible plants you can use in your greenscape.

Take advantage of green's many hues

These two landscapes rely on green plants, not on brightly colored flowers, for variety. **Left:** *Volcanic rocks, low stone wall, concrete paving accent green still life of sedum, Japanese maple, river birch. Design: Frits Loonsten.* **Right:** *Side yard holds multihued collection of evergreens for year-round beauty. Some are dwarf varieties; these will retain size, shape with little pruning for several years.*

...Picture Gardens

Sheltered courtyard for people, shade-loving plants
What was formerly 500 square feet of dirt became a
cheerful garden just off the living room. **Top:** Covering the
fenced area is a trellis to hold louvered aluminum screens.
Screens shade ferns, ornamental asparagus, and baby's
tears ground cover, also make deck a more comfortable
place to sit. **Left:** Pump carries water to top of small
waterfall, where it splashes down stone steps into pool.
Evaporating moist air helps make the garden ideal for
shade-loving plants. Design: Mary Gordon.

...Picture Gardens

Houseboat gardener takes a most audacious approach

When your living quarters are an especially small space, it's only natural that your garden will follow suit. Here, containers are crowded into all available outdoor space around houseboat. These on railing are surplus rifle boxes. Containers used hold at least a 6-inch soil layer. They're covered with 2-inch-mesh chicken wire to prevent cats from digging and ducks from nesting in them. Premixed soil comes in 10 and 35-pound bags; 100 pounds fill a large container.

Who would think that traffic is just outside the wall?

Privacy is easy to come by on this secluded,11-foot-deep front patio off the living room. Reclaiming a portion of the front yard for private use, block wall effectively shuts out the sight of passing cars and people. Container-planted chrysanthemums rest on basketweave paving. Irregularly shaped podocarpus provides interesting plant accent. Strong lines of partial overhead cast intriguing patterns on ground. Bench encourages side-by-side seating.

Choosing Shrubs for Small Spaces

In the small-space landscape, shrubs have many uses. They can provide privacy as hedges or dense, green walls, or they can serve as boundaries defining specific areas. They can soften the structural lines of houses or fences. Or shrubs can be used alone as specimen decorative plants, showing off flowers, fruit, or interesting foliage.

The shrubs listed below all work well in small spaces. Your local nursery or garden center will carry the variety of each plant that grows best in your climate. Be sure to specify that you want the compact or small form, since some of these plants come from large families that produce sizable varieties.

Aucuba. Evergreen. Shade. Many variegated forms. Needs ample water; tolerates many soils. Hardy to 0°F.

Azalea. Evergreen and deciduous. Most like partial shade; Southern Indica types are vigorous and prefer full sun. A wide range of flower color and blooming season.

Barberry. Evergreen and deciduous. Likes sun. Can be grown to 7 feet. Evergreen to −5°F. Make good hedges.

Boxwood. Evergreen. Sun or shade. Many varieties. Commonly used for hedges and edgings. Can be clipped into formal shapes.

Camellia. Evergreen. Give some sun. Many varieties; can be upright growing or spreading. Profuse bloom in white, pinks, corals, reds from winter to late spring. Prefers acid soil.

Cotoneaster. Evergreen and deciduous. Likes sun. Can have upright or spreading growth. Flowers are followed by red or black fruit.

Cypress (Chamaecyparis). Evergreen. Either sun or shade. Most have compact growth; some are spreading. Foliage varies from bluish green to yellow green to gray green.

Euonymus. Evergreen and deciduous. Likes sun. Upright and spreading varieties. Some have fall color.

Forsythia. Deciduous. Sun. Plant shape depends on variety; grown for yellow, spring flowers on bare branches. Rest of year, medium green foliage blends with other background shrubs. Use as screen or espalier. Hardy in sub-zero weather.

Heather. Evergreen. Likes sun. Low, spreading growth. Flowers come in white, pinks, red.

Holly. Evergreen. Either sun or shade. Small varieties resemble boxwood. Likes slightly acid soil. If you want berries, the safest way is to plant both a male and a female plant. Berries may be red, orange, yellow, or black.

Hydrangea. Deciduous. Likes partial sun. Big, bold foliage and flower clusters in white, pink, red, or blue (under some conditions). Flowers are long lasting. Effective when massed in partial shade or planted in tubs on a patio. Prune to control.

Juniper. Evergreen. Likes sun. Many varieties with upright, bushy, or spreading growth. Needlelike foliage with fleshy berrylike cones. Will grow in any soil.

Nandina. Evergreen. Sun or partial shade. Delicate foliage with some leaf color. White flower clusters may be followed by berries. Resembles bamboo, but not invasive. Hardy to 0°F.

Oregon grape. Evergreen. Sun or shade. Glossy or dull green, oval, spiny-toothed leaves; scattered mature red leaves through year, more pronounced in fall. Spring flower clusters; blue-black edible fruits with gray bloom. Hardy in sub-zero weather.

Podocarpus. Evergreen. Sun or shade. Narrow, upright growth; easily pruned to shape. Hardy to 10°F.

Potentilla. Shrubby forms are deciduous. Likes sun. Small, mostly single, roselike flowers, cream to bright yellow, white, or pink, in summer. Very tolerant of poor soil, heat, drought.

Privet. Evergreen or deciduous. Likes sun or shade. Abundant clusters of flowers in late spring, early summer, followed by berries. Widely used as hedges, or clipped into formal shapes and featured in tubs or large containers. Fewer flowers will appear on clipped hedges or shaped privet because most get trimmed off.

Pyracantha. Evergreen. Likes sun. Glossy leaves, bright berries. Plants have thorns; grow out of pathways or patio areas. Can be pruned into shapes or espaliered.

Rosemary. Evergreen. Sun. Dark green aromatic foliage; blue flowers. Will tolerate hot sun, poor soil; needs good drainage. Hardy to 0°F.

Viburnum. Evergreen or deciduous. Likes sun or shade. Clusters of flowers, often fragrant, and clusters of berries. Some forms have fall color.

Yew (Taxus). Evergreen. Sun or shade. Slow growing. Conifers that bear fruit instead of cones. Tolerant of much shearing and pruning. Good for hedges, screens, or in containers.

City Gardens
Skyscrapers don't cancel out plants

A city garden? Does this seem like a contradiction in terms? Not so. Its urban setting makes a small, gemlike garden all the more delightful.

There will be problems, of course—neighboring high-rise apartment buildings that create perennial shade; smog; and intensified winds that seem to seek out open, planted spaces. But the determined city gardener will accept the challenge of creating an oasis surrounded by buildings, streets, and vast expanses of concrete.

Forming the mainstay of many city gardens, gardening in containers is both versatile and practical. Gardeners who rely on containers for most of their gardening can control soil quality, keep plant care to a minimum, and rearrange their landscape for frequent variety. Almost any plant can be grown in a container. And containers let you rotate seasonal color and readily replace plants past their prime.

The specialized techniques used in container gardening are discussed on pages 56-57.

Tower'd cities please us then,
And the busy hum of men.
    L'Allegro, John Milton

Dealing with the Problems

Shade, smog, and wind are the most common troublemakers a city gardener will have to face. The effects of each of these problems can be lessened by choosing plants that will do well in a given situation.

Intense shade, usually caused by tall buildings on all sides, is the real light problem in most city gardens. The best method of dealing with constant shade in these artificial canyons is to grow such shade-loving plants as fuchsias, begonias, ferns, impatiens, or azaleas.

Plant selection also helps solve the smog problem. The smog that hangs around many large cities can be deadly to plants, clogging pores in leaves and creating a toxic atmosphere. Some plants—ivy, oleander, azaleas, ginkgo, camellia, and privet—

Several Victorian row houses share garden court
Each unit in row housing has deck that looks out on garden court at basement level. Brick-on-sand paving for play area, generous gardens are features. Design: Douglas Macy.

This balcony holds a tucked-away garden

Compact second-story balcony off apartment living room was transformed into outdoor seating area. To include some plants in design, slim, white, custom-made plant pedestal with shelf that holds potted plants at eye level (containers are hidden) fits behind chairs on far end of balcony. Pink and white fibrous begonias provide summer flowers; summering house plants sit on yellow cube tables. Design: Alan Day.

Party space expands to lower patio on spiral staircase

Townhouse owners needed expanded entertaining space off second-story living room. A spiral staircase was the answer. **Left:** *Wide balcony off living, dining rooms is good for sunning, shelters lower walkway. Trees, shade are borrowed from nearby yards.* **Right:** *Impatiens-lined spiral steps lead down to yard, back gate. Design: Robert C. Chesnut.*

Plant shapes, bold paving make strong design statement

Ferns, camellias, boxwood surround jasmine arch. Island contains holly, azaleas, pittosporum.

...City Gardens

fight smog better than others; let these hearty survivors form the foundation of your garden.

Wind can be a problem anywhere, but especially on high-rise balconies or decks. Plants for windy gardens should not require staking or have long, heavy branches. Begin with small plants, so they can adapt as they grow. Good plants for windy gardens include holly, ivy, boxwood, euonymus, pyracantha, cotoneaster, geraniums, and junipers.

Wind screens or baffles may also be a workable solution. For further information, see page 7.

Creating Private Space

In some city gardens, neighbors live so close that total privacy will be impossible.

One good solution will be to hide your garden behind a fence, garden wall, hedge, or small tree. When curious onlookers live above you, a patio roof, cover, or awning will give you some seclusion.

Geraniums color up hillside home balcony
To modify all-wood look, small area along deck's edge was filled with gravel, outlined with header board, to display container plants: geraniums, lobelia. Gravel lets pots drain without staining deck; can be watered down to increase humidity. Design: Wallace K. Huntington.

Planter boxes follow zig-zag line of brick terrace
Petunias, marigolds, other summer annuals gaily outline narrow penthouse balcony 16 stories up. Terrace has just enough space for an intimate party. Planter boxes put a plant's width between railing, guests for safety.

This small garden suggests romance
Green city garden almost requires a moonlight stroll. Design called for repetition of circles: first circle is far, sedum-edged fountain off small garden room; second takes form of geranium, caladium beds encircling sundial. Mixture of brick, slate paving adds variety. Design: Loutrel Briggs.

These City Gardens Use Every Inch of Space

Reclaimed front yard becomes private space

Once a bare rectangle of grass, walled front garden offers fountains, terraced beds, space off living room for party overflows. Terra cotta color tones repeated in brick paving, brick edging on raised planters, fence, plant containers, flower colors. Statue, clay finials add to formal air.

European influence pervades rear garden

Reminiscent of formal French gardens, rear garden is totally private. Italian cypress line brick walls. Symmetrical beds filled with marigolds, trimmed boxwood surround central fountain. Garden access is through loggia off kitchen, dining room.

Another view of rear garden

Cantilevered and angled overheads partially roof colorful enclosed courtyard. Folding glass doors close off loggia during inclement weather. Plantings on balcony and in lower garden include marigolds, lobelia, geraniums, and boxwood shaped as topiary. Statuary, containers, garden furniture set the predominantly formal style of this fanciful garden scene.

In this small city lot (40 x 60 feet), the only way to gain some private outdoor space was to totally enclose it. The house, garage, and driveway occupy much of the space, leaving room only at front and back for small gardens.

Both the front and back gardens reflect the personality established inside the house. They create spaces for entertaining that seem to flow naturally from indoors to the open air. Both gardens provide the only outdoor views for the adjoining rooms. And, like twins, the two gardens share similar features—classical statues, fountains, formal flower beds, topiary, identical plants and furniture. Only close inspection reveals the delightful differences.

In the front garden, a fountain sets the mood. Double glass doors in the living room open to the garden, frame the view, creating a vibrant mural that changes with the seasons. Both doors open wide to steps leading down into the garden, almost doubling usable space for entertaining. Around the perimeter terraced raised beds form planting areas for annual flowers and closely cropped boxwood. The stately dracaenas (the palmlike trees that flank the statue) and larger, three-tiered topiary grow in large containers. A central fountain, set flush with the flooring, and matching benches complete the landscape.

At first glance the back garden appears quite formal with its precisely even planting beds and careful balancing of elements. But the bright yellows, oranges, reds, and greens in the plants, cushions, and wood trim make this outdoor space exciting and contemporary.

The kitchen window, at one end of the loggia, opens onto a wide ledge, perfect for serving food and drinks buffet style.

Transformed from an uninspired back porch, the loggia offers transition space between house and back garden. Large, glass bifold doors can be closed to create an indoor garden room during inclement weather or opened wide to accommodate a flow from the house into the garden.

Above the loggia on the second story, a private balcony becomes still another outdoor space. The canvas overhead, frequently needed for privacy and shade, can be pushed back for sunbathing.

In order to achieve this harmonious blending of house and garden, every square inch of the lot was needed. Before you try this approach to your space squeeze, though, check your local building codes for setback and height restrictions.

Design: W. David Poot.

...City Gardens

Lath, deck, salvaged skylight combine to transform patio area
A festive 20 by 30-foot entertaining area is topped by recycled industrial skylight in lath structure over service, dining area (left). Overhead view (right) shows open-air deck, woodburner on tiles. Mandevilla vine climbs arches. Design: Richard Lesnick.

Cascading plants can bring a balcony to life
On tiny 6 by 12-foot balcony, plant boxes atop 3-foot-high panels cascade with petunias. Design: Richard W. Painter.

A meticulously planned, intimate hillside garden
Lawn patch off dining room deck framed by L-shaped bench extension of lower step. Design: Mr./Mrs. Peter Vismanis.

Put Some Plant Color in Your Small Space

For bright spots in the small-space garden, plant flowers. They provide colorful accents—grown in borders, hanging baskets, containers, or mixed in with ground covers or low-growing shrubs—for your patio, balcony, deck, or any other garden area.

In small spaces, most gardeners rely on flowering annuals for their color; a few perennials also fill the bill.

Bulbs can be a problem in tiny spaces. They have a short blooming season, usually in late winter, spring, or early summer. And once their bloom is spent, the remaining foliage should be allowed to die back naturally. This dying foliage can be an eyesore, unless it is concealed by a ground cover or annual plants.

If you feel it isn't spring without some tulips or daffodils, try forcing bulbs in containers; these can be whisked away once the bloom is spent.

Annuals bloom for one season, then die. Where winters are mild, plant spring blooming annuals in the fall. In other climates, plant them in early spring. Plant summer blooming annuals after the last frost. Since most small-space gardens are subject to close scrutiny, you should buy already established plants from a nursery or garden center. Doing this gives you an instant display.

Perennials produce new growth at the beginning of each growing season, then bloom for varying periods of time throughout the year. After blooming, plants are left in the ground where they produce more foliage or die back until next year. Though it may be difficult to hide fading or dormant perennials until their next growing season, some have flowers that make the effort worthwhile.

Nurseries and garden centers will carry flats or individual containers of established plants or seedlings when their appropriate planting season arrives.

Alyssum. Annual. Likes sun. Blooms spring, summer with white, lavender, purple, or rose-colored flowers. Spreading. Good in containers, hanging baskets.

Begonia, wax. Perennial. Likes partial shade. Summer, fall flowers in white, red, pinks.

Candytuft. Annual. Likes sun. Blooms in spring in white, pastels. After first bloom, shear top lightly to stimulate new growth.

Chrysanthemum. Perennial. Likes sun. Blooms in summer, fall. Many flower forms and colors. Pinch back main stems for bushiness, continuous bloom. Available all year in bloom; buy these and use as accents.

Coleus. Annual. Likes sun. Grown for spectacular foliage, usually several colors to a leaf; has inconspicuous flower spikes summer, autumn. Foliage color becomes more vivid in strong, indirect light. Use high nitrogen fertilizer, give plenty of water. Cuttings root easily in water.

Daisy, Marguerite. Perennial. Likes sun. Blooms summer, fall. Yellow and white flowers. Makes good cut flowers. Best in mild winter areas.

Geranium. Perennial. Likes sun. Blooms in spring, summer, fall. Versatile; easy to grow. Ivy geraniums good in hanging baskets. Best in mild winter areas. In cold winter areas, take cuttings for next season.

Hosta. Perennial. Likes shade. Attractive, heart-shaped foliage. White or lavender flower spikes rise to 2 feet above plant. Dies back in winter.

Impatiens. Annual. Likes partial shade. Blooms in summer; showy, often bicolored flowers in white, pink, red, orange.

Lobelia. Annual. Likes sun. Blooms spring through fall; tiny blue or purple flowers in low, spreading mounds. Good as an edging or in hanging baskets.

Marigold. Annual. Likes sun. Blooms in summer in yellow, orange, rust, near-white.

Nasturtium. Annual. Likes sun. Blooms in many colors in summer, fall. Easy to grow from seed. Some trailing types will climb a trellis.

Nemesia. Annual. Likes sun. Blooms in spring in wide range of brilliant colors. Needs rich soil, cool spring weather.

Pansy. Annual. Likes sun. Blooms in winter, spring. Compact plants with large, multicolored, flat flowers.

Petunia. Annual. Likes sun. Long lasting, trumpet-shaped flowers in summer; comes in all colors but green. Trailing Cascade series good in hanging baskets.

Primrose. Annual or perennial. Likes shade. Blooms in late winter, spring. Brilliant or pastel, long-lasting flowers on tall, sturdy stems.

Stock. Annual. Likes sun. Blooms in spring; very fragrant flowers in white, red, pink, blues, purple. Makes good cut flowers.

Verbena. Annual. Likes sun. Flat flower clusters in summer in a wide variety of colors. Resists heat.

Zinnia. Annual. Likes sun, hot weather. Blooms in summer in wide variety of colors, sizes. Subject to mildew.

Spaces Shared with a Neighbor
Cooperation leads to bigger gardens

Some small-space gardeners have discovered a novel way to expand their outdoor living area—they share space with their neighbors.

Sharing can be done in two ways: two or more neighbors can connect their individual small spaces to create one large outdoor living area, or a garden can be visually expanded by "borrowing" part of a neighbor's landscape without jeopardizing any privacy.

Whichever way you choose to share, you'll need to plan carefully. Sharing space with other people requires a clear understanding of how the space will be developed and maintained.

If you wish to share space that is owned collectively—such as private space that is adjacent to commonly shared areas in a condominium or apartment unit—check with the management before you include this common land in your landscape plans. They may have plans for this space that you are unaware of.

'Tis need that tests one's neighbors.
  Peer Gynt, *Henrik Ibsen*

Joining Forces to Expand

When two or more small individually owned spaces are relandscaped into one large, shared garden, all the people involved need to agree on several points: how the space will be used; how materials, plants, and necessary labor will be purchased; and how the large garden will be maintained.

Usually the idea for sharing space arises from a common need. Several parents may want to increase play space and provide built-in playmates for their small children. Or people in apartments, condominiums, or city houses that have adjoining small garden areas may want to make better use of their tiny spaces by combining them.

Frequently one unifying design element will be needed to visually tie the small spaces together. A large wooden deck or patio area, a generous walkway that leads guests to the various houses, or a large patch of lawn or ground cover can provide the unifying key. Smaller, private areas can be screened by hedges, dense foliage, fences, or baffles.

Legal matters should be considered, too. You will want to check with your local building department or building code to see what restrictions you will need to follow. It's also wise to ask your insurance company whether or not your present liability insurance policy covers the new situation; it might be necessary to purchase a group policy.

How to Borrow Scenery

One of the principles of Japanese landscaping is "borrowing" scenery from a neighbor. Few small-space gardens contain large trees. But if your next-door neighbor has a large tree, you can "borrow" it visually by planting smaller trees near it so the eye will include the whole group of trees. Instead of fences or walls, you can plant a hedge or dense shrubs: solid structures tend to stop the eye, but green plants tend to lead your vision out to the surrounding area.

A word of caution: if you plan your design around a neighbor's plants or trees, you would be wise to discuss your ideas with him before proceeding. His future landscape plans might make what you intend to do in your space a wasted effort.

Condominium's patio is partly private, partly public

Just off kitchen, living room, small-space patio was surrounded by large lawn, shared by everyone in complex. To gain some privacy yet avoid boxed-in feeling, part of area was fenced, part left open to lawn. Bright pink oleander softens outer fence. Design: Philip S. Grimes.

Sharing neighboring greenery—one of the secrets of Japanese landscape architecture

Left: *View from covered terrace off living room shows ornamental side garden with stones bridging pond, bench, stone lantern, bamboo fence. Background maple, pine trees are partially borrowed from next yard.* **Right:** *A perfect garden for meditation. Design: Hoichi Kurisu.*

Row of cypress block view into entry from street
Sliding glass door opening to apartment's cinder-block patio is home's main entryway. Since stockade fencing was only waist high, cypress shield doors, create leafy view. Design: Mark Holeman.

Property ends at tree, garden continues up hill
Small patio area at rear of house ends just beyond dogwood tree. Instead of fencing patio in, hillside was left open to visually increase space. Design: William Kapranos.

Circular hideaway with an old-world patina
For a completely different look in a standard townhouse patio, design called for circular central patio paved with flat fieldstones, unusual arched fountain on shared wall has sculptured bas-relief that sends sheet of water into pool. Small trees, shrubs line edge of walls, fence. Stone walk continues on to back gate. Design: Dick Ammon, Ted Gantz.

...Shared Spaces

Double the problem, double the pleasure

Since both small outdoor areas were visible from living room, designs had to work together. **Top:** *Basketweave brick paving, built-in benches share space with entry.* **Right:** *Back patio has wooden decking, raised planters for citrus, shrubs, flowers. Design: Roy Rydell.*

Close-up plant view—through glass

Potted impatiens fill tiny ledge. Design: R. David Adams.

Dealing with Driveways, Sidewalks, and Parking Strips

Needed for utility but often short on beauty, driveways, sidewalks, and parking strips pose a problem. Their paved, unplanted look can add a jarring note to a landscape design. To soften such a broad expanse of pavement, you can carve out tiny sections to create pockets for plants.

Since driveways provide vehicle access from the street to your garage or carport, any planting must be kept out of the traffic. You can plant along both sides of the drive or, as is shown below, create small planting beds in the center. This also visually breaks up the large expanse of paving.

Sidewalks and parking strips can be effectively bordered by plants. Or, portions of the walk can be removed and made into flower beds. If a fence or wall is adjacent, plants can cascade over the top.

Since these spaces are so tiny, keep planting simple by concentrating on one or two plants to avoid giving the area a cluttered look.

Inventive ways to banish that bleak parking lot look
Plants often take a back seat in landscaping planning for sidewalks and parking strips. Here are some exceptions. **Top:** *Exposed aggregate paving in driveway relieved by green planting islands of ivy, trees. Design: Robert C. Marvin.* **Bottom left:** *Shingled fence, stone retaining wall draped with poppies, alyssum, other spreading plants. Design: Robert W. Chittock.* **Bottom right:** *Poppy-filled sidewalk cutout at base of light post adds color.*

...Shared Spaces

Neighbor's trees enhance multilevel garden
Adding to charm of raised-bed plantings in this garden is view of neighbor's foliage rising behind low fence. Stylish shingled eyebrow tops fence. Walls, steps are cobblestones. Design: William Hendricks and Raymond Biondi.

Plant proportions increase apparent space
Artfully grouped around rustic stairs leading to elevated entry, plants are scaled for maximum effect. Eye travels from standard azalea in pot at foot of steps to small, potted bonsai pine, then to large, tubbed pine.

Wide entry shares benefits of street trees
New patio of scavenged bricks makes wide, handsome entry to house, also offers a spot for sunning and entertaining. Street trees beyond privacy screen at left offer greenery, shade.

Index